# THE
# BLUNT
# PLAYWRIGHT

# THE BLUNT PLAYWRIGHT

## AN INTRODUCTION TO PLAYWRITING

## CLEM MARTINI

### SECOND EDITION

**PLAYWRIGHTS CANADA PRESS**
TORONTO

LIBRARY AND ARCHIVES CANADA CATALOGUING IN PUBLICATION
Title: The blunt playwright : an introduction to playwriting / Clem Martini.
Names: Martini, Clem, author.
Description: Second edition.
Identifiers: Canadiana (print) 20190166762 | Canadiana (ebook) 20190166770
| ISBN 9780369100191 (softcover) | ISBN 9780369100207 (PDF)
| ISBN 9780369100214 (EPUB) | ISBN 9780369100221 (Kindle)
Subjects: LCSH: Playwriting—Textbooks. | LCSH: Drama—Technique—Textbooks.
| LCGFT: Textbooks.
Classification: LCC PN1661 .M28 2019 | DDC 808.2—dc23

Playwrights Canada Press acknowledges that we operate on land, which, for thousands of years, has been the traditional territories of the Mississaugas of the Credit First Nation, Huron-Wendat, Anishinaabe, Métis, and Haudenosaunee peoples. Today, this meeting place is still home to many Indigenous people from across Turtle Island and we are grateful to have the opportunity to work and play here.

We acknowledge the financial support of the Canada Council for the Arts—which last year invested $153 million to bring the arts to Canadians throughout the country—the Ontario Arts Council (OAC), Ontario Creates, and the Government of Canada for our publishing activities.

 Canada Council Conseil des arts
for the Arts du Canada

 ONTARIO ARTS COUNCIL
CONSEIL DES ARTS DE L'ONTARIO
an Ontario government agency
un organisme du gouvernement de l'Ontario

 Canada

 ONTARIO | ONTARIO
CREATES | CRÉATIF

# CONTENTS

# CONTENTS

## CONTENTS

# CONTENTS

CONTENTS

# CONTENTS

**Part Ten: Epilogue**

# WELCOME

Welcome to the second edition of the *The Blunt Playwright*.

I initially wrote this book over a decade ago when I realized how thoroughly colonized Canadian theatre remained, even after decades of notable, homegrown, work. In Canadian classrooms, libraries, and bookstores you could find any number of texts on the topic of playwriting, but not one that employed regular exemplars written by Canadians. It was as though Canadian playwrights and playwriting had never existed.

I embarked on a search, found—of course—that there was no shortage of terrific Canadian plays to draw from, and so set out to create a text that used examples from many countries, including Canada.

Since the book was first launched, however, many things have changed. The technology employed in the profession is probably the most noticeable aspect. It was, for example, standard at one time for a playwright to slip their brand new script into a brown envelope and mail it to a potential producing theatre. Now, although some theatres continue to require a hard copy, the majority request electronic submissions. At the same time, adaptations and improvisational approaches to playwriting have gained greater currency. This second edition attempts to reflect these changes.

As might be expected, new and exciting plays have been written since *The Blunt Playwright* first hit the bookshelves. I've included scenes from several recent works in this edition.

As well, I received feedback from readers that found the writing exercises included in the book enormously useful, and consequently have added a couple more to the roster.

Over a decade after having written *The Blunt Playwright*, I remain convinced that there is no livelier, more genuinely human form of writing than playwriting, and this book continues to offer the same message about the writing process that it did when it was first released. There are no easy routes to success; no secrets, no rules, no shortcuts. There continues to be only one way to find your way to the audience and that is to write your way there.

So enjoy the process, set your fears aside, and get busy.

# WARNING

There are thousands of books out there on writing. If you are naive enough to believe that by simply reading a book, any book, you will suddenly become a writer, you are sadly mistaken. If you picked up this book with that end in mind, stop reading now.

Close the book.

Slip it back on the shelf. Walk away.

# FURTHER WARNING

If you're still reading, it can be assumed that it's because you believe that writing is an art that requires study, thought, and hard work.

Good.

That being said, there are many, many people out there who believe that the road to happiness lies in writing. They believe that by writing a play they will become rich. Or famous. Or rich and famous. And then they will become happy.

This is also nonsense.

In the lofty hierarchy of the theatre, playwrights appear very low on the totem pole indeed. Producing artistic directors rule the theatres and so control the purse strings. Playwrights are hired, perform their necessary duties, and are sent packing. And in the great overarching hierarchy of the entertainment industry that embraces theatre, film, television, novels, and interactive gaming technology, theatre is the poor country cousin. Film and television writers make infinitely more money, novelists are accorded infinitely more international esteem and recognition, and writers in the interactive gaming field exist in a whole other dimension of cool. So if you hope to upsize your budget or ego by becoming a playwright, stop reading now.

You're still reading, so it's reasonable to assume this is because you are interested in playwriting and in writing in general, and that you want to know more about the craft. It's fair to assume you are willing to work hard, because much of any success that you may achieve in writing—most—is dependent upon how hard you are willing to work.

# INTRODUCTION

When reading about playwriting it's easy to assume that the craft crawled from the steaming primordial murk of prehistoric storytelling, evolved by stages through the Greek and Roman ages, quickly loped through the Shakespearean and the Shavian eras, and finally walked erect and fully formed into a modern age dominated by British and American writers.

The largest concentration of English-language play-producing theatres exist in America and Britain respectively, and theatres in those countries are most inclined—naturally enough—to produce works written by fellow American and British citizens. Consequently, the majority of contemporary plays written in the English language are of American or British origin.

And yet there are interesting and important works being written the world over. If these works don't make their way to mainstream American or British stages, that doesn't make them any less vital.

I've tried to include examples of plays from a variety of international sources in this book. At the back I've included a reading list. This isn't meant to be a comprehensive or exhaustive compilation—merely an interesting place to begin an examination of the kinds of plays that have been, and are continuing to be written, in this enormous global village of playwrights.

# PART ONE
## A BLUNT
## DISCUSSION

# PLAYWRITING
# IS DIFFICULT

There are some who will attempt to persuade you that playwriting is easier than you think.

I'm not one of them.

It's not particularly difficult to develop an understanding of the structure and theory of playwriting—that can probably be learned by a relatively smart individual with access to a good computer—but like figure skating, while one may understand things very well theoretically, the real trick lies in learning to execute that technique in a reliable manner, time after time, without doing injury to yourself or others.

Here are three things one can safely say about playwriting.

## 1. *There Are No Secrets*

Everything you need to know about playwriting and storytelling is in plain view. The winds of time have eroded the soil that the body is embedded in and the bones are exposed for everyone to see. Anything said here, in this book, can be confirmed or denied simply by getting up and taking the time to wander over to the local library to read some plays.

In fact, I recommend doing this in any case. One of the best and most useful things you can do if you want to learn about playwriting is to read broadly and deeply.

## 2. *There Are No Rules*

There exists a large body of advice regarding the writing of plays. It has an ancient and distinguished lineage, dating back at least as far as ancient Greek civilization. But in the end, there are no rules—and no policing body to enforce them, even if there were.

Writers tend to be contrary, cantankerous, and opinionated. For every piece of advice given, you're likely to find someone who objects. That's fine. A little contrariness can be invigorating. But you disregard this body of practice entirely at your own risk.

## 3. *There Are No Shortcuts*

People sometimes ask how they can become a writer quickly. Well, you can't get there from here.

There's nothing quick about writing. And in many ways it's an unreasonable request. Would one ask the same question if one was pursuing a career in, say, surgery? There is no "quick" route to success in any serious endeavour. Writing is a life-long wrestle. Sometimes you're on top. Sometimes it is.

The upside is this—if it were only a wrestle, eventually you would tire. But, luckily, writing is a paradox as well. Though you draw from it, it gives something back. The longer you work, the harder you work, the truer you work, the more it has to return.

# WHY "BLUNT"?

According to my dictionary, one of the definitions of "blunt" is "plain-spoken and abrupt." Frankly, the craft of playwriting can afford some plain speaking.

There's been a lot of writing regarding playwriting that isn't plain. Some of it is long-winded and convoluted. Some of it is wrong-headed, or just plain nonsense.

As for abrupt, that seems eminently suited to the craft of the playwright, situated, as it is, perpetually in the present. It's a type of writing that lends itself to spare treatment, with little room for excess or overstatement.

Sounds blunt to me.

This book won't tell you everything about playwriting. Can't. Won't even try. What this book will attempt to do is edify, clarify, and demystify. And through it all I will try to be as simple, direct, and blunt as possible.

# SOME GENERAL GUIDELINES

*1. A Play Presents a Vision of Life and Draws from Life*

Life is the real deal, and we are all simultaneously participants and observers.

Everything we know, everything, comes from life, either as direct observations and thoughts or through the filter of someone else's. One of the best things one can do as a writer of any kind is to observe closely and participate fully in life, because it provides you with a template for your material.

*2. The Best Instructor of Writing is Writing*

This is so obvious one is almost tempted not to mention it. Before there were writing teachers, writing manuals, expensive writing retreats, coaches, clinics, dramaturgy, writing theory, or writing workshops—there was writing. If you are serious about becoming a writer, then write. It's that simple.

Sit down. Start now. Maintain a daily routine and don't stop. The writing itself will teach you things if you let it. Writing is simultaneously very complex and very simple. The craft requires a synthesis of internal emotions and impressions and a keen understanding and observation of others. It requires brevity and distillation.

So write. In fact, I would submit that the most serious indicator that someone is genuinely interested in writing is if they have been unable to stop.

The opposite is also true. There are many people who talk a good game as writers but are unable to start.

The bitter medicine every writer must swallow is that the cure for most writing ailments is continued practice. If you wish to improve as a writer—write. If you wish to better understand the writing process—write. If you wish to get beyond fear and writer's block—write. It's tough, astringent medicine, but, sadly, it is the only cure.

### 3. The Second Best Instructor of Writing is to Give it Away

The moment you give others your writing to read, your writing will begin to improve. The reason for this is at this point you begin to truly concern yourself with communicating.

While you write for yourself only, your writing need only be good enough to entertain yourself. There may, however, be serious gaps in your writing that, because you are the writer, you are unable to see. What isn't on the page, you subconsciously fill in. The moment you let others read your work, the writing must say it all, and say it well.

### 4. The Third Best Instructor of Writing is to Get Over Yourself

Giving it away is only useful if you are then able to listen carefully to those who read your work. It means humbling yourself. It means not becoming defensive. It means understanding and being able to embrace the fact that you will sometimes be disappointed. Accept the critique and move on.

### 5. It is Essential That You Listen. But Don't Listen Equally

Why? Because some people are bone ignorant and others are well intentioned but misguided. Choose your reviewers carefully. Select people whose opinion you respect. That doesn't mean you should choose only individuals who will express unadulterated adoration of your work, however. Find people you can trust and then after they have read your work, sit still and listen.

*6. Develop an Effective Critique Filter*

As a beginning writer you must quickly develop a finely tuned, carefully calibrated critique filter or you will find yourself hip deep in steaming guano very promptly. There is plenty of bogus advice out there that passes for knowledge and if you simply accept it, you can spend years chasing your own tail.

I studied with one instructor, who shall remain nameless out of regard for their progeny and the burning humiliation they might feel, whose most singular word of advice on playwriting was—and this is a direct quote—"If you wish to become a playwright you must board a bus for New York City at midnight with no money in your pocket. Take the bus to the heart of the city. Get off."

And if that were the only bit of bad advice out there, things would be much, much easier for the young writer, but there is simply tons of that kind of inept, lazy advice.

People make rules, often people with more time on their hands than is healthy. Ignore them. Stay sane. Keep writing.

*7. Playwriting is Writing and You Write on Your Own. Theatre on the Other Hand is a Miraculous Act of Co-operation*

When you write your play, most of the work is done on your own. You can request advice, you can attend readings, but the work is done largely by placing your behind in a chair and firing up the computer.

That being said, when you finish your script you are still a long way from the end of the road. A script is only a blueprint for production. In a very real sense it doesn't truly exist until it is performed, and that final stage requires the skills and talents of many, many people—designers, directors, actors—and before that script gets up on its feet it will have to move through the creative filter of each of these individuals.

That journey from page to stage will require your attention, your protection, and, through it all, clear communication. It's not a pristine art form, it can be messy, it can be painful, and sometimes you'll find yourself turned upside down. That's the risk you take—and half the fun.

8. *There is No Room for Delicacy in Playwriting*

Playwriting is a noisy, irreverent, crowded art form. It requires that you develop a kind of callus upon your soul. One must deal with egos of the most outrageous sort, and, contrary to popular opinion, actors are not the worst offenders. Directors, producers, designers, agents, and stage managers—these disciplines all have their share of individuals with egos of a very robust sort. If you are inclined to be delicate, be forewarned.

# FEAR

*We think we know ourselves, when we really know only this little bitty part. We have this social person that we present to each other. We have all these galaxies inside of us. And if we don't enter those in art of one kind or another, whether it's playwriting, or painting, or music, or whatever, then I don't understand the point in doing anything. It's the reason I write. I try to go into parts of myself that are unknown . . . I'm not doing this in order to vent demons. I want to shake hands with them.\**
—Sam Shepard

There's a colourful assortment of impediments writers must confront on the way to producing their work, but fear is probably the scrappiest and most difficult to overcome.

There's no time and really not much point to delivering a stirring homily about courage, but let me say this. I've taught playwriting to university students and I've taught writing to kids in trouble with the law, and there were plenty of things that set them apart, but they were in exactly the same rickety, teetering boat when it came to being white-knuckle afraid of exposure.

Often, novice writers worry that they have nothing to say. Well, even a two-year-old has *something* to say. It's not having nothing to say that impedes writing. Rather, it's the concern that there is nothing to say that doesn't carry enormous risk. People fret that they'll be found inadequate, won't be funny enough, interesting enough, intelligent enough, quirky

---

\* Susan Letzler Cole, *Playwrights in Rehearsal: The Seduction of Company* (New York: Routledge, 2001), 12.

enough, deep enough, cool enough, talented enough. Won't be—fill in the blank—enough.

Because whatever you write, it's going to say something about *you*. Your choices, your understanding of character, your view of the world, your sense of humour, your belief system. You. Your DNA is carried in every dot and dash of the sentence and story structure. And there's nothing to be done about it, really—except to understand this. In the end, although a perceptive audience may detect you through your writing, the majority of them don't want to. Aren't interested. Couldn't care less. That's not what they've come for.

They haven't come to collect biographical information. They've come for the story, and most times, while they may catch the odd glimpse of you, dimly, between and behind the lines on the page, they won't care.

So lay your fears aside, throw caution to the wind, and get busy.

# PLAYWRITING IS CREATIVE WRITING

There is the curious impression floated by some folks, who have more time than is good for them, that there is one kind of writing that we'll call creative writing, which generally includes poetry, prose, and certain types of creative non-fiction.

Then there is this other kind of writing, a more technical kind, that, hunched over, simply limps about and shoves words into rough narrative stacks that a talented director and a scad of actors then sort through, repair, burnish, and erect—at which point the shaggy stack is miraculously transformed into a genuine play.

Well, that's just demented.

I believe this misunderstanding arises because playwriting is so often taught in the theatre department of post-secondary institutions rather than in the English department along with the other creative writing forms. This separation, while understandable (playwrights tend to want to linger near the stage; they know that's where the action is), skews and warps what should be the common ground between the forms.

The truth is, that when one is writing a play, one is both creating and writing. That makes playwriting, by definition, creative writing. And one is creating pretty much everything, every time. Through efficient, thoughtful, dedicated attention to the content, style, tone, plot, dialogue, and characters, one creates an entire world when one writes a play.

Those who reduce playwriting to something more technical, some lesser form of writing that requires only that one heave certain rough-hewn narrative blocks around, misunderstand the form. The limitations placed on playwriting are no greater than the limitations placed on any literary genre. That is to say, there are nearly none.

If proof is required, simply trot to the nearest library and pick up a few texts that exemplify the variety and scope that exists in playwriting. *Rhinoceros* by Ionesco. *Romeo and Juliet* by Shakespeare. *Death and the King's Horseman* by Wole Soyinka. *Fool for Love* by Sam Shepard. *Top Girls* by Caryl Churchill.

Of course, the opposite of all this is also true. If playwriting is about more than just assembling things into a kind of rough order, then that means the playwright is responsible, truly responsible, for all the words and deeds, and then there is no lifeguard watching the beach, no ranger scanning the woods from the fire tower, no director or producer or actor waiting to rescue the errant playwright. The script, and all its attendant trials, the rewrites, the edits, workshops, and subsequent rewrites, become the playwright's responsibility.

# THE WORLD AS IT WORKS

Before picking up the pen, however, it's worth considering the word "play" for a moment.

Short decades ago, "playing" was thought of as something only children did. It was considered a whimsy—unimportant and trivial. Likewise, theatrical plays and presentations have long been regarded as a form of light recreation. Artists have often been characterized as a sort of lesser species of children, perpetually playing, caught in an advanced form of seriously arrested development.

However, notions about play have changed considerably. It's now believed that the activities once regarded as playful and slightly shallow are instead important and meaningful to human development. Through "playing" children acquire the physical and emotional skills necessary to become fully functioning adult human beings.

Likewise, it's possible that storytelling is also a much more vital and integral part of being a human than was previously thought. Language appears to be something that is genetically programmed into humans. That is, we are predisposed to learning to talk in the same way we are predisposed to learning to walk. It's not a far stretch to believe that we are hard-wired for stories as well. After all, from the time we learn to talk, we also learn to use and shape stories.

Children at an early age are able to understand the structure of story. They have a very perceptive command of sequence and are able to determine when a story has come to completion. "And is that the end?" they ask, intuitively sensing that a complex pattern has been fully realized.

Stories allow us to more fully understand the world. In a sense, it doesn't matter that listening to stories is a pleasurable activity, any more than playing is a pleasurable activity. It's possible that it is pleasurable in the same way that so many necessary things are pleasurable. Eating. Being warm. These things are essential to our existence and consequently we register the fulfillment of these essential requirements as pleasurable.

Some people view narrative structure as a series of invented contrivances that a network of artists have invented and then imposed.

I don't buy that.

It seems to be more likely that a play is an extension of something humans have done, and perhaps were equipped to do, from the day we were born.

Rather than believing that plays and the structure they employ are derived from a series of arbitrary notions created by a mysterious cabal of professional writers, this book will assume that there are elements of playwriting that are natural, logical, and even necessary. That the structure of plays is in part guided, not by rules, but by how we as humans communicate with one another.

With that in mind, I will draw upon not just what has been written about plays, and can be discerned by studying plays, but also by what we can draw upon and observe in real life.

It is relatively easy to understand that the subject matter contained within a play is based upon those things we have observed in our lives—but I would take this a step farther and propose that many of the structures and mechanisms of playwriting are ones that are drawn from our lives as well, and I will be referencing this later when we discuss structure.

Simply put, just as sharks have been created to swim and devour slower and smaller fish, humans have been designed to consume (and generate) stories.

# WHAT YOU NEED TO KNOW ABOUT STORY YOU PROBABLY ALREADY KNOW

If one proceeds from the notion that *narrative* is an essential, integral part of being human, then it also follows that we probably enter the world as equipped to build narrative as we are built to walk or talk. It's clear that we consume stories eagerly from the time we first try to understand the world. We begin structuring stories almost as soon as we begin to talk. From that time on we use stories every day.

Ask someone what happened during the day, and chances are good that she will frame parts of it as a story.

Maybe it will go something like this:

**YOU:** How were things at work?

**SHE:** I don't want to talk about it.

**YOU:** Why? What happened?

**SHE:** My supervisor is driving me crazy. He's completely out of control, like crazed-elephant out of control. There's no reasoning with him, it's like he can't hear. He hears the words, but it's another language, a language he never bothered to learn, the language humans use—look, I'm sweating!

**YOU:** Do you want to sit down?

**SHE:** If I talk about this another second I'm going to have to kill something, and you're the only other live thing in this room, so it might be you.

**YOU:** Maybe you want to talk about it later.

**SHE:** No, no, I'll be okay. *(takes a deep breath)* He told me that my department has got to do ten percent more work with five percent less budget. I told him that can't be done. That's morally and mathematically impossible. He gave me his written plan that he said showed it was possible. I couldn't make any sense of it. I mean, I couldn't make any sense of it. It's like a work of fiction, it's like he gave me a fairy tale to read. I said, I can't use this. He asked me what I was saying. I said, this isn't a business plan, this is science fiction. He said, I should talk with him in his office. I was steaming at this point and went after him . . .

I won't pursue this any further, but you get the picture. Even in a short portion of this improvised scenario one can recognize the rough elements of narrative structure. There's a "setting-up" portion in which the grieved speaker attempts to establish the principal characters: Who they are. What they want.

There is an "introduction of conflict" and a definition of what that conflict is. The struggle develops from there and intensifies. One can already sense that a confrontation and climax is in the offing, and, following that, some kind of resolution.

This form, this structure, this way of shaping and understanding things, can be detected almost anywhere within human interaction. Ask a child returning home from school how their day went, listen to people recounting their holiday adventures—chances are that portions will fall within this paradigm.

In the end, to understand someone or something fully, one must place them into a context. Story *is* that context.

So, when one approaches playwriting or storytelling, it's not so much learning these things from the beginning—because you *already know them*. It is more about being aware of skills you already possess from a lifetime of practice and honing them.

# A PLAY IS A
# CONVERSATION

For instance.

There is a lot to be learned about playwriting simply from observing your average conversation. For one thing, in some respects, a play mimics conversation. People talk on stage, both to themselves and to others. Dialogue is often the element that comes easiest to the beginning playwright, and it is the thing that tends to set playwriting most obviously apart from other forms of narrative. The audience sees real live people, really conversing with one another.

But in another and perhaps more important respect a play *is* a conversation, a particular kind of conversation. It is a conversation between the playwright and an audience. Each play represents something the playwright has to say in this ongoing conversation.

If you want your audience to listen, then you will have to pay attention to the (until now) unwritten conventions of conversation.

In any good conversation there are several qualities that the interested conversationalist attempts to execute:

1. Ensure that you are ADDING TO THE CONVERSATION. What new information is being brought to the dialogue, or, what new way of examining old information?

2. AVOID REPETITION. Nothing is more annoying than when people repeat endlessly what they have already said, again and again and again.

3. MAKE SENSE. This seems obvious, but how many times in one conversation or another have you seen someone lose track of what they were saying? Perhaps the speaker gets ahead of himself. Perhaps he, or she, fails to draw things together. This same sort of thing can happen when one writes plays, with the same deleterious effect.

4. GET TO THE POINT. If what you are saying is important, folks are always willing to allow you time to develop things, but patience isn't infinite.

5. Remember that time you got LECTURED, AND HOW YOU HATED IT? That's true in playwriting as well.

6. LET THE TONE OF YOUR CONVERSATION BE GUIDED BY THE CONTENT and the person you are addressing. When one is telling a joke, the tone is different than if one is discussing the death of a family member. Likewise, if you are addressing a close friend you will use a different tone than the one you would use if you were addressing a business associate.

7. Above all else—DON'T BORE. For many years I performed with an improvisational theatre group. It was a convention in those performances that if an improviser became too tedious, a judge seated in the front rows would hold up a large cardboard sign with a zero inscribed on it and shout, "Warning for boring." The improviser would then be removed from the stage. Probably the most inspired idea ever. And, oh, how often have I wished I could apply this strategy in real life. A simple truth that one should understand about writing is this—the audience won't wait for the next brilliant idea if you bore them. They won't reward you. Even if they don't hold up a sign and holler "warning for boring," they will be wishing that they could.

# BUT SOMETHING
# ELSE IS GOING ON
# IN THE THEATRE

It can be argued that all the literary arts represent a kind of dialogue between the artist and a particular audience. But something special sets theatre apart. It has real live people on stage, and a group of real live people silently watching in the seats. And the question one has to ask is, why do we all go sit together to watch a play?

Beyond the commercial exigencies of the contemporary theatre that require a certain number of paying heads to pay the rent, and the salaries of the professionals involved in the production, there is something else, and something important happening. *The audience is part of the experience.* Not just as spectators, but as true, active participants.

It's worth noting that the audience also listens to and observes the audience. Actors know very well that it is harder to make a small audience laugh, because a large number of people laughing provide a sense of permission.

A play is, in a sense, a laboratory. It is a testing ground. What is being tested? Perhaps it is the essential accuracy of the writer's vision. A writer proposes a theory.

He or she says the world is like this. But of course, anyone can *say* something and be wrong. The audience is the polygraph test. The audience's reaction informs the actors, but it also, and much more importantly, informs the audience.

Someone laughs in the audience, and it confirms just what I, as a member of the audience, was thinking—that something amusing has happened. Someone confesses a painful secret on stage, and the utter silence that fills the theatre informs me that the others seated next to me also find the confession compelling and truthful.

The audience surrounds you and provides you with information. If you laugh, and everyone else laughs, you understand instantly that the feeling you have about that scene is not something unique to yourself—it is a feeling that is shared by others. The vision of the writer is assessed, moment by moment, by the audience, in this most unique testing ground.

The final response of the audience determines whether a truthful vision has been presented . . . or not.

# ARISTOTLE

It's impossible to discuss playwriting without devoting at least a paragraph or two to Aristotle.

Aristotle was a Greek thinker and teacher who lived from 384 to 322 Before the Common Era (BCE). He wrote on a number of topics including philosophy, biology, psychology, logic, politics, and the arts. As thinkers go, Aristotle rates pretty highly. He had a keen mind and a fine pedigree— he was, after all, a student of Plato and supposedly a teacher of Alexander the Great. When one discusses structure today—all these many, many years after his death—he continues to be quoted and referenced as much as anyone. His discussion of **plot** and **character** in the *Poetics* still have the capacity to shed light on the workings of the theatre, as it does in the following passage, "The first principle, then, and to speak figuratively, the soul of the tragedy, is the plot, and second in importance is character . . ."[*]

But there are several problems that occur when one utilizes Aristotle's analysis in contemporary discussions. For one thing, he just lived so long ago. It's difficult to bridge the historical gap between then and now, and to give one an idea of just how wide that gap is, he was writing his poetics when comedy in the theatre was still a relatively innovative development. It had only really been introduced a short hundred years earlier, around 486 BCE.

---

[*] Leon Golden, translator, and O.B. Hardison Jr., commentary, *Aristotle's Poetics: A Translation and Commentary for Students of Literature* (New Jersey: Prentice-Hall, 1968), 13.

For another thing, it's worth keeping in mind that he wrote in another language—not just Greek, but ancient Greek. This isn't the language you'll find spoken today in a grocery store in Athens, and contemporary translations of ancient Greek sometimes differ. As O.B. Hardison Jr. says in his commentary on the *Poetics*, "Then there is the problem of translations, but a translation is always a disguised commentary. Even the most conscientious and well-trained translator makes innumerable choices when rendering a passage of the Greek into English, and his choices depend heavily on assumptions he makes about the larger meaning of Aristotle's argument."[*]

Finally, since Aristotle was among the first to attempt to describe some of these thoughts about art and theatre, the terminology he used is difficult to grasp because he was also inventing it as he went. So, when he wrote about "the imitation of the action," the contemporary reader may find themselves scratching their head, and should realize that scholars during Aristotle's time may have scratched their heads as well.

Likewise, when Aristotle spoke of drama "purging the emotions," one has to understand that this was Aristotle's best effort to describe a phenomenon that is, by its nature, difficult to capture in words.

It's astonishing, and a measure of just how crazed things can get, that in this day and age, people still argue about terminology, swap antique Greek terms, and speculate if something can genuinely be categorized a tragedy if the play does not meet the obscure standards established in the fourth century BCE.

Instead of tying ourselves into knots trying to determine if theories written concerning ceremonies performed thousands of years ago have application to theatre today, we may want to step back a moment and breathe.

Aristotle's writings on action and structure are still useful. But let's just remember that anything written by Aristotle, or by *any* theoretician for that matter, should be provable through our own contemporary observations. What can't be tested and proven should, like any theory, be set aside.

---

[*]  Golden and Hardison Jr., 55.

# SHAKESPEARE

It is simply unavoidable that another corpse be exhumed and examined when one studies playwriting. The cadaver in question is that of William Shakespeare.

Unlike Aristotle, Shakespeare wasn't a theoretician. Shakespeare was a player. There exists no writing of his that attempts to explain or analyze playwriting, but nevertheless much of what we understand about drama today comes from our collective study of Shakespeare's canon.

Now, for one as famous as William Shakespeare, there's surprisingly little known about the man. We know roughly when he lived and where he lived. On pretty much every other matter, things are open to debate. There's even an ongoing argument about whether the fellow we know as "Shakespeare" actually wrote the plays that bear his name.

Theories attempting to explain who the real Shakespeare was are legion and head-scratchingly abstruse. One hypothesis, for instance, holds that it wasn't Shakespeare who wrote *Hamlet*, but another person by the same name. Another theory maintains that Shakespeare was merely a paid front man for the real writer who preferred to write prolifically, but anonymously.

Nor are we absolutely certain that every play that exists in Shakespeare's canon was written by Shakespeare. There are a number of plays that it only constitutes the best guess that the plays are his, and just to demonstrate how reverentially some people treat him, there are those who argue passionately that a number of the plays credited to Shakespeare

are so badly written that they could not possibly have been written by Shakespeare.

One thing beyond dispute, however, is the effect that Shakespeare has had on drama. After the Bible, Shakespeare's plays are the most widely read works in the English language. They have had the most impact upon the English language as well. Just consider for a moment all the words, phrases, images, and characters that have become part of everyday usage as the result of Shakespeare. The names Romeo, Juliet, Shylock, Falstaff, Macbeth, Hamlet, Brutus, Lear, Portia, Ophelia, and Othello have all been endowed with iconic qualities and are referenced every day. Phrases first penned by Shakespeare such as "to be or not to be," "lend me your ears," "the qualities of mercy," "my pound of flesh" are echoed in print, on screen, and in casual conversation. One simply cannot turn about without running into the enormous thumbprint left by Mr. Shakespeare.

Shakespeare remains the most produced playwright in the English language and the most easily marketed. One doesn't have to travel far to find a festival or professional theatre or a series performed "in the park," "by the beach," "in the ruins" dedicated to his work. He has become the gold standard that all playwrights are held up to.

In no other genre is any one writer as revered, as omnipresent, as dominant as Shakespeare is in contemporary Western theatre. There is no comparison that exists in the novel form, or in film, poetry, painting, or sculpture. There are even Shakespearean plays that have been translated into text message, so that his plays can be sent and studied via cellphone. As a consequence, when discussing playwriting, it's enormously useful to reference Shakespeare's work, because knowledge of his canon spans cultures and ages. In this text, for instance, I'll be using certain of Shakespeare's works to illustrate structural issues or concerns for the obvious reason that if one wishes to make a point about structure, one can feel a degree of certainty that people who are interested in playwriting will at least be familiar with some of the Bard's more popular plays. Shakespeare's work has morphed over time into a kind of cultural shorthand.

This is at least partially true, because enormous amounts of money are spent teaching Shakespeare in schools and ensuring that every citizen has access to their democratic share of the Bard of Avon. It is perhaps for this reason that the influence of Shakespeare is found on so much contemporary work. *Kiss Me, Kate; West Side Story; Goodnight Desdemona (Good Morning Juliet);* and *Rosencrantz and Guildenstern are Dead* are just a few of the contemporary reworkings of the Shakespearean canon, and if one scratches the surface of any number of plays one can find echoes of his writing.

There's no doubt that Shakespeare was a very talented playwright, nor is there any doubt that his works still have the capacity to move a modern audience, but along with this contemporary adulation comes a troubling legacy.

There was a period of time some short while ago when it was common practice among Christians of a certain persuasion to pose the question, "What would Jesus do?" whenever they were confronted with a difficult moral conundrum. In the theatre, "What would Shakespeare do?" has become the equivalent question posed when one confronts an aesthetic dilemma.

That the most produced playwright in contemporary times is a man who has been dead for hundreds of years is both unsettling, and a little sad. In the end, one of the unintended effects this fervour for Shakespeare has had is to transform the theatre into a bit of a museum. Young people, who may never have attended a play by a contemporary writer in their lives, are often summoned to pay their respects at the Shakespearean House of Wax.

This completely distorts the function of theatre. Rather than operating as a medium of communication and discovery it instead becomes a mechanism of cultural improvement, rather like attending an expensive finishing school.

And there are other disturbing side effects. Theatre, more than any other form, with the possible exception of opera, is considered by the general public to be the genre of an elite crowd. One may simply attend a film without enrolling in any advance training. One may sit down in one's living room in one's bathrobe to watch television. In the theatre, there is the feeling that even if you are not actually going to see Shakespeare you may be required to have some understanding of his works. Keep the Coles Notes handy, we are cautioned, just in case a pop quiz is delivered.

As the contemporary theatre attempts to attract a more diverse, multicultural audience, at the same time it sends several distinctly negative messages. One clear message is that the most produced and popular playwright is a dead, white male writing in an antique, difficult to comprehend form of English. If you wish to enter, the theatre says, here is your first test.

If the contemporary theatre is to evolve and reach out to a larger audience, one thing it must do is shake off these remaining vestiges of ancestor worship.

Shakespeare was an artist with tremendous talent—no doubt—but he also held many of the prejudices of his times, and even as a writer he was completely fallible. He had good and bad days.

When you are having a rough time writing and don't feel you have the ability or skill or anything to say, it's worth meditating on how Shakespeare must have felt when he looked back at the terrible failings of *Timon of Athens*.

And then consider that he recovered from that and went on to write *The Tempest*. Now, that's inspiring.

# ONE LAST WORD
# OF WARNING

Many texts end up saying something like this: the theatre is hungry for good scripts, and if you build a better play, the world will beat a path to your door.

That's patently untrue. It's worth reflecting on the fact that the previously referenced historical figures were both male, and both of European origin. That's no coincidence.

The long, long history of playwriting has been dominated by males of primarily European heritage. Even a very quick scan of the canon will reveal that there are comparatively few female writers. For an extended period of time it did not matter how well you wrote. If the subject matter, or the playwright, did not fall within certain prescribed limitations, the play would remain unperformed, the playwright unproduced.

In their book *Plays By and About Women*, editors Victoria Sullivan and James Hatch note that, "In the theatre, financial backers have been loath to risk the large amount of money necessary to mount a play by a woman in a society where patriarchal attitudes have reigned in relative security until recently."*

Something of a similar nature can be said regarding the difficulties faced by playwrights of colour. During my time as president of the Playwrights Guild of Canada, I often heard members of minority groups

---

* Victoria Sullivan and James Hatch, editors, *Plays By and About Women* (New York: Vintage, 1973), vii.

list the many reasons provided by the artistic directors of theatres for being unable to present their particular plays. The stories, they were informed, appealed to too small a demographic.

The plays were too specific, too limited, too marginal. They didn't fit the theatre's mandate to entertain. They wouldn't appeal to or reflect the experiences of the subscription audiences. They would prove too expensive to produce due to the necessity of auditioning and hiring an out-of-town cast.

It can be discouraging to attend play after play and not find your history, your gender, your culture, or your point of view represented. It makes it difficult to create art when there isn't the same kind of historical precedent to draw upon, or some sense that your point of view is honoured and celebrated.

That being said, the world has changed, is changing, and there is every reason to believe that the extent and pace of that change will increase. There are many excellent female voices to be found in playwriting, as well as many extraordinary writers from non-Western, non-European backgrounds. The audience is more diverse than it has ever been, and there is a need and a genuine yearning for new visions, new stories, new voices.

# PART TWO
## STRUCTURE

# STRUCTURE

*You ask me to tell you how a play is made . . . One day a long time ago, when I was scarcely out of school, I asked my father the same question. He answered: "It's very simple; the first act clear, the last act short, and all the acts interesting."* *
—Alexandre Dumas, fils

*Whether you like it or not, the first thing you have to worry about when you're working up a story is its framework.* **
—Anton Chekhov

In the same way that not all books at the library are novels, not all theatrical events you attend are plays. It is entirely possible to arrange an entertaining, exciting, thoroughly worthy evening in the theatre without putting a single play on the stage. A musical revue, for instance, can be entertaining—but it's not a play. Likewise one could assemble a charming evening of literary readings, perform it before an audience, and still not have presented a play.

Musical revues, dance, performance art, readings—the theatre is large enough and malleable enough to embrace and celebrate all these activities. But it's not useful or accurate to describe these activities as plays, any more than it would be useful or accurate to call a dictionary a novel

---

\* Brander Matthews, *Papers on Playmaking* (New York: Hill and Wang, 1957), 85.

\*\* Anton Chekhov, "Anton Chekhov on Writing," Study Lib, https://studylib.net /doc/8482619/anton-chekhov.

because it has a hard cover. Though they may each have pages and lines filled with words, they manifest different structures and accomplish different goals.

So, with the intention of being accurate, in this book a play will be considered a specific kind of narrative that is written for the express purpose of being performed live by actors. There are several elements that are more or less essential to animated narratives of this kind.

# STRUCTURAL ELEMENTS

## DESIRE

When you craft a play, you are not really crafting it from words, sentences, or even thoughts. Instead, you dip your playwright's pen into a well filled with something much more elemental than ink: you dip it into *human desire*.

Everything we learn in a theatrical narrative we learn as characters act upon their very specific, very selfish, sometimes conscious but often unconscious desires. When these desires have been fulfilled, or perhaps to the contrary these desires have been well and truly rebuffed, then there is nothing left to write. You have no remaining material. Your play is over.

## CONFLICT

Conflict: perhaps the second most potent element of drama. Novice writers often object to the notion that conflict is integral to the dramatic form. Not all life is based on disagreement, they contend. Won't that simply assure that the play will be a negative experience? Can't we all just get along?

But if a play is about presenting a true vision, there must also be a mechanism that permits that vision to be tested for truth. If someone makes an artistic statement that life is a certain way, shouldn't one expect proof?

**Struggle** (and I think struggle is a more appropriate term than conflict) supplies that proof—a particular kind of proof that the audience can evaluate through their own discreet observation. Seeing, after all, is believing.

How important are the desires of these characters? How effective are the strategies they pursue? The audience will come to their own conclusions as they watch the characters strive to achieve their objectives.

Galileo's struggles in Bertolt Brecht's play of the same name reveal the inventor to be fallible, but tenacious. Brutus proves himself to be essentially honest, but capable of self-deception. Willy Loman's life principles are proven to be flawed, and Willy himself is found critically, fatally unable to adapt.

These struggles allow us—the audience—to perform our own discreet investigation. Many of the thoughts and ambitions that humans hold are held in reserve. Hidden away. Struggle forces those ambitions to rise to the surface. As the conflict escalates, it compels characters to move beyond safe and easy solutions. It forces the characters to reach deep into their hidden reserves. In this way, struggle renders the invisible visible and allows the audience to understand the characters in a new way.

# BEGINNING, MIDDLE, AND END

Life is infinite. A story is a subset of life, and finite.

We writers draw upon life for all our major symbols. (There are some that object and point out that writers also draw upon the unconscious, which is true; but what does the unconscious draw upon if not life?) We observe the world and try to discover patterns of meaning. But life is so truly complicated and vast that it can best be understood in digestible portions.

Every story, then, has a place where it starts and a place where it ends, and this implies that for all but the very briefest of stories there is a middle as well. Even if the story is told in a non-linear, fragmented, abstract fashion, it must still begin somewhere, and conclude somewhere.

Okay, so it seems obvious then . . . beginning, middle, end . . . every story exists within this frame. One of the first critical decisions a playwright must make is in the selection of where to begin the play, and precisely where, and how, to end it.

# THE ACTIVE AGENT

A story must be about someone, and in theatre more than any other medium, the story is propelled by the actions of that particular somebody.

In the novel, the audience is privy to the intimate thoughts and musings of the writer. The writer guides the reader on their journey through a direct conversation, and the words they write are the compass directing the reader through that journey. In film, the audience is presented images captured by the camera, and the story is propelled forward at least partially through the delivery of those images.

In the theatre, the audience understands the narrative almost entirely through following the decisions made and choices taken by the actors.

The theatre operates on a couple of relatively simple equations. No actor = no action. No action = no story.

# SETTING

Every story happens somewhere and somewhen. Even if the story occurs in an abstract space, that's somewhere. And the "somewhere" and "somewhen" of that story impact upon every other element of the play. Could *Cyrano de Bergerac* occur in any other place or time than France in the seventeenth century? Could the events of *A Raisin in the Sun* occur anywhere else but post–World War II America?

So, with those five elements in place: **Desire** as the fuel, **conflict** as the engine, **time** as the frame, the **actor** as the driver, and the **setting** as the road, you are then prepared to fire up the motor and set out.

As a rule, I don't do graphs.

There are many charts and maps and graphs that have been drafted to describe plays, some of them very complicated. If making a graph helps you visualize your story, by all means draw one up. If having a lump of coal on your desk (as I did once when I was writing a play set during a coal mining disaster) helps you, place it there.

But I defy anyone to find a single writer who has ever written their play moment by moment *according to a graph!*

I have read texts that had charts that were much more complicated, but I have never known anyone to actually use one. In my opinion, if you see something that looks like this—

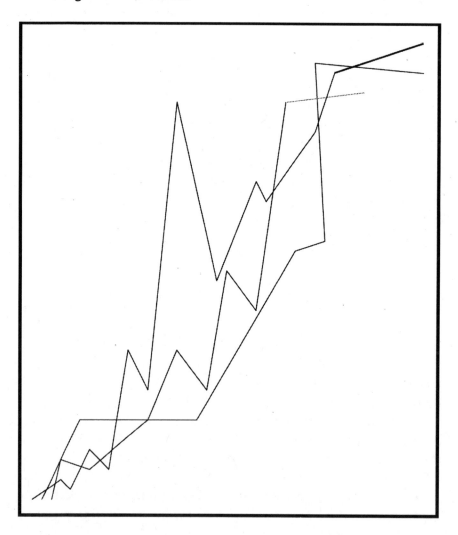

—put the book away. You have picked up someone's ECG.

As far as I'm concerned, a graph can only serve as a rough visual aid for discussion purposes, and this is about as complicated as it needs to get.

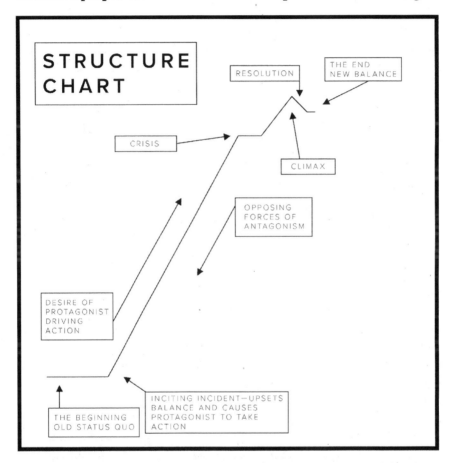

There are a couple of things that are made very clear when you look at a graph of this sort.

Once again, we are confronted by the elegant finite nature of the play.

There is a beginning and an end. The beginning must, by its very definition, have some kind of impulse that separates it from all the other things that happened prior and which will provide the energy for the ensuing action. This is most often referred to as the **inciting incident**.

The esteemed British director Peter Brook once said all one needs to perform is an empty space. Well, without an actor all you have is reams and reams of empty space to look at, so someone must drive the play. That person (or occasionally a group of people) is referred to as the **protagonist**. The protagonist is neither good nor bad by definition, but is simply the person whose desire provides the forward driving energy for the play.

Resistance to the protagonist's desire is most often generated by a human agent, and that person (or group of people) is most often referred to as the **antagonist** or antagonists. The antagonist isn't necessarily bad or villainous. The antagonist is simply the individual/individuals who most opposes the action.

The play climbs—that is, the motion of the action is one which continues to escalate throughout. This is often referred to as **rising action**. It operates on **conflict and struggle**—that is, in a sense, the action of the piece surges uphill against an equally powerful force. It is through this struggle that your characters are truly revealed, and it is within the context of this struggle that your story is framed.

This middle portion of the play is often characterized by **complication**. What that means is that the protagonist at one point or another perceives a problem and pursues a course of action to remedy the problem. Unless that action is immediately successful—and it can't be unless the play is very, very short—he/she will encounter an unexpected reaction. The reaction will be stronger than anticipated, or different than anticipated, and it will compel the protagonist to take stronger, or different action. So the action moves from simple and direct to something more complex and intense.

The actions of the protagonist move from those things which are easiest to achieve to those things that are most difficult. This too mimics real life. If I'm thirsty, I suppose I could slake my thirst by first divining where groundwater exists, digging a well, pumping up the cool liquid, and pouring myself a glass. But in all likelihood my initial impulse might be to walk to a sink and turn the tap on. Humans tend to attempt the easiest solutions first. When they are thwarted, they then move to explore solutions that require more energy, effort, and thought.

Shortly before the graph ends, one encounters the **crisis**, or the moment when the protagonist, having already applied many strategies to achieve their goal, is forced to choose a final course of action. This is followed shortly by the **climax** when the opposing forces hang in the balance. This is the moment of greatest intensity and most complete revelation and it is toward this moment that the play inexorably moves. The climax is the last of a long series of interconnected struggles and it is only generated when all other possible strategies and options have been exhausted. Consequently, it can also be characterized as the moment of greatest testing. Is your protagonist capable of fulfilling their ambition, or are the forces they face too powerful? Ultimately this question is answered—and more than answered—demonstrated, by the climax.

The ending swiftly follows because the job of this story has, in a sense, been completed and the desire that fuelled the play in the first place has been expended. There is nothing left to do except to demonstrate the impact of these actions. What, of significance, has resulted from this struggle? What does the world look like now that these forces have met? These moments are normally referred to as the **resolution** or falling action.

Again, the graph is not a talisman. It has no magical properties, nor is it meant to prescribe how every play should be drafted. It is meant only, in a very general way, to offer a visual representation of the process of playwriting.

# A CASE STUDY

I've chosen the following short play to dissect as a way of further exploring structure.

It is selected because it is in every way a minnow-sized text. Small and compact, all its many bones near the surface; one can fillet it and examine it in its entirety in a very short time. Let's proceed.

## *GUPPIES* BY CLEM MARTINI

*Two guppies swim behind a large plate of glass. They nudge the glass and swivel in the water for a few moments.*

**EVA:** You want to mate?

**ELDON:** No.

*Pause.*

**EVA:** You want to swim down to the concrete castle at the bottom of the aquarium and nibble lichen off it?

**ELDON:** No.

*Pause.*

**EVA:** You want to swim back and forth along the edge of the glass?

**ELDON:** Uh uh.

**EVA:** Those tetras treat the fern as if it were their very own. They're so selfish. I bet if we went down together we could chase them away. Do you want to, Eldon? Chase the tetras away?

**ELDON:** God, you make me sick. If only you could see yourself. Eat, sleep, mate, chase the tetras.

**EVA:** What's the matter with you? You never want to mate anymore. We never go down to the gravel and stir up the murk looking for bits of food that have dropped to the bottom. I used to love stirring up the murk with you.

**ELDON:** It's over between us, Eva. I'm in love with Big Face.

**EVA:** *(laughing nervously)* Don't be silly. The Big Face doesn't know we exist.

**ELDON:** Of course she knows we exist. She looks at us all the time. She's got such big, gentle eyes.

**EVA:** You can't be serious. She lives outside the tank.

**ELDON:** You want to know what I see when I look into those eyes? The capacity to do something other than just mate, sleep, and eat, Eva. She has that delicate nose. Those sensitive lips. You don't have lips.

**EVA:** Be reasonable. Fish don't have lips. You don't have lips.

**ELDON:** She looks so intelligent, I know she would say interesting things if we were to talk together.

**EVA:** And she's enormous.

**ELDON:** That just shows how shallow you are. Even if she was a thousand times larger than she is, and I was a thousand times smaller, I would still love her. Can you understand that?

**EVA:** Think. She lives outside the aquarium. How could you meet her?

**ELDON:** I've been studying the air pump. When the tank has fresh water poured in, the air bubbles pop right up near the edge of the tank. Fresh water was put in today. If I were to follow in the slipstream of one of those bubbles right now, it would carry me out.

**EVA:** But you wouldn't be able to breathe.

**ELDON:** I've been training up along the surface, exposing my gills to the air, slowing down my metabolism. I can last for hours now, without a single breath of water. And, if I were to attach a few mucous balls of water near my gill slits, it would allow me an even longer passage of time.

**EVA:** And then what? A few hours, a few feedings, it's all the same. You need water.

**ELDON:** I'd either be rescued or not. My fate would rest with Big Face.

**EVA:** *(sadly)* You've planned it all out, haven't you?

**ELDON:** Nights, when you all would hover motionless near the branches of the fern, I'd slip down to the bottom of the tank, pile gravel on my back, and do push-ups. I can walk on my fins now, Eva.

**EVA:** *(simply)* I love you.

**ELDON:** You don't love me. It's just the genetic coding driving you to spawn. Big Face will be here soon. I'm going to meet her.

**EVA:** There's nothing I can say? I'll miss you.

**ELDON:** You won't miss me for long. You're a guppy through and through. Besides, there are plenty of other fish in the tank. Goodbye.

*ELDON swims off. EVA hovers. Another fish approaches EVA—IVAN.*

**IVAN:** What's Eldon doing down by the air pump?

**EVA:** He's going to meet Big Face. There he goes over the edge.

*We hear the sound of ELDON popping out of the water, followed by the sound of him landing on the floor beside the tank.*

**ELDON:** *(off)* I'm out! I'm out!

**IVAN:** He must be mad.

**EVA:** Here comes Big Face.

**ELDON:** *(off)* Hello, Big Face! I have escaped the fish tank! I love you!

*We hear the deafening sound of a cat mewling with pleasure, followed by ELDON's shrill scream.*

*(off)* Yaaaa!

**EVA:** Will you look at that?

**IVAN:** I'll be a son of a gun.

*A moment of silence passes as they digest the extraordinary events.*

You want to mate?

**EVA:** No.

**IVAN:** You want to go eat some minnows?

*Pause.*

**EVA:** Sure.

*IVAN and EVA swim off together.*

*The end.*

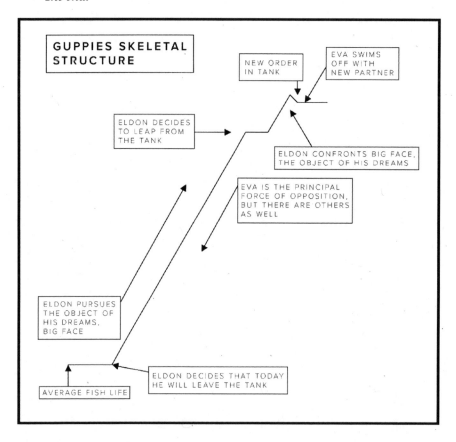

**WHO**

So, let's first identify the players.

Eldon is the **protagonist.** Why? He's not especially heroic, he's argumentative, overly emotional, he jumps out of the fish tank and is swallowed by the thing he is supposedly in love with. And, of course, everything he believes so deeply in is wrong.

But he is the protagonist because he *desires* something and he *acts* upon that desire, and the desire has sufficient scope that it can form the spine of this particular story.

WHAT

What is it that he wants?

It's clear that he wishes to escape the tank and meet Big Face—proving, if it ever needed proof, that the desire of your protagonist need not be a rational one.

WHERE DOES THE OPPOSITION RESIDE?

Who is the **antagonist**? Eva is. Not because she's an especially villainous, bad, or wicked fish. In fact, she has many good qualities: common sense, a good grasp on reality—better than Eldon's. But, as smart and as sensible a fish as she is, she manifests the principal forces of resistance toward Eldon and his scheme, and that is all that is required of her—or anyone—to make them the antagonist of a story.

What have we got between these two fish, then? Struggle. Strife. Heat. Eldon wants to go. Eva wants him to stay. Something has to give. Conflict results.

Every play has it. Every play needs it.

BALANCE—THE STATUS QUO

What is the initial status quo of this story?

All the guppies exist inside the fish tank, some happy, some not, but it's certainly a fish's life—as usual.

THE INCITING INCIDENT

Something happens to disturb the status quo. In this case it's Eldon's readiness to leave the fish tank and meet Big Face. Once he has achieved that state of readiness he feels compelled to act upon it.

## THE CONFLICT

The protagonist acts as a result of the inciting incident. In this case, as soon as Eldon believes he is ready to leave, he takes his first action. He confronts his fish lover, Eva, and informs her of his desire to meet Big Face.

## RESULTING ANTAGONISM

If Eva had simply acquiesced and said goodbye, there would be no struggle, no story, and no mechanism to investigate the characters. Instead, the agent of antagonism, Eva, resists the actions of the protagonist, Eldon, with all the forces at her disposal. She argues, pleads, reasons with Eldon, mocks his plans, and finally confesses her love in the hope that he will be dissuaded.

## ESCALATING CONFLICT

The arc of the play is one of **rising action**.

Observe how the strategies utilized by Eldon and Eva grow increasingly demanding. Initially passive, Eldon merely ignores Eva. He only elects to confront her when it's clear that she won't leave of her own volition. Eva chooses to bare her fish's soul to Eldon and risk the pain of rejection only when it is clear that nothing else will work.

## CRISIS

Every argument met, all other choices made, Eldon must put up, or shut up. He decides to pursue the course of action that will enable him to confront the object of his desire. He follows the bubbles up and out of the tank.

## CLIMAX

The two premises, "I must go and live my dream" and "your dream is impossible, stay with me," are in such a degree of conflict that an impasse is reached and something has got to give. Eldon escapes the tank, confronts the object of his affection—Big Face—and is compelled at the same time to face the horrifying truth.

RESOLUTION AND RESULTING NEW STATUS QUO

Everything in the tank finds itself living within a new status quo following this struggle. Eva finds a new and more practical lover, one eminently more suited to her character. The tank is finally purged of foolish dreamers—and life proceeds relentlessly on.

WHAT IS AT STAKE?

This decision—to stay in the tank or leave—is of vital importance to the protagonist of the story, and ultimately it has life and death consequences.

If the story is not important to the characters on stage, it probably won't be of any consequence to the audience either.

THEME

There's a theme within this tale, as there is a theme to be found within every complete story. I suppose in this case it's something in the nature of "curiosity killing the cat." But the theme emerges out of the story, rather than directing the plot. And generally that is the case, the theme emerging from the story, rather than the other way around.

# CHARACTER VS. PLOT

This is where an oft repeated and completely disingenuous controversy generally arises. Boiled down, it demands that you choose which is more important—character development or narrative structure. This is akin to being asked to decide which is more important, consonants or vowels.

Character and structure are inextricably, unavoidably intertwined. Characters are informed and shaped by story, which in turn generates the decisions and choices that create that particular sweep of narrative.

To place this in some kind of perspective, here is a short exercise you can perform. Think of adjectives that might most effectively describe Eldon. Now, find proof within the text to justify the descriptor you've selected. Perhaps you find him "inventive" (he does, after all, construct an intricate plan to leave the tank). Maybe you find him "irrational" (he refuses to pay attention to the very real dangers associated with leaving the tank). Or perhaps you find him "romantic" (he appears to be ruled by his heart in his decision to leave the tank).

Apply the same exercise to Eva. One might describe her as "practical" (she perceives, rightly, that fish need water). Maybe you find her "caring" (she attempts to prevent Eldon from making his rash, ill-conceived decisions).

*All* those adjectives, *all* those elements that we discover about character arise not out of things said about Eldon or Eva—there's remarkably little said about either of them—but, rather, out of *actions* taken. In other words, these elements of character emerge out of plot.

The struggle that the characters are plunged into acts as a crucible that in its white-hot heat, shapes and defines them.

# AN ADDITIONAL WORD ABOUT CONFLICT

Conflict can be defined most simply as a struggle between two opposing forces. In a play, the conflict that holds the greatest potential, and therefore the greatest interest for the writer, is that conflict which exists between the principal forces of the protagonist and antagonist; however, there are other secondary arenas of conflict. In general, one can say that a play is propelled moment after moment by and through conflict.

Conflict may be present on a number of different levels within a single play. Conflict may exist between the protagonist and the antagonist, as well as between the protagonist and other opposing characters. Conflict may exist between the protagonist and less obvious forces as well—between the protagonist and society, for instance, or between the protagonist and the environment. And it is always possible that there may be conflicts striving within the protagonist.

Conflict should not be confused with mere argument, however. If two characters bicker endlessly, it doesn't really matter that they are in conflict because it results in a relatively static exchange. "Did not," "did too," and their equivalent do not advance a story because they don't change or add to the essential information already received by the audience, and they don't alter the essential balance of power between the characters.

Nor does activity equal action, no matter how flamboyant or seemingly theatrical. A character may skip, sing, draw a gun, strip naked, chew gum, and knit a warm, wool toque all at once and still not advance the story in any essential manner. Dramatic action is only that action which attempts to promote a character's interests and desires against an opposing force.

# PART THREE
## GETTING ORGANIZED

# WHAT IS TO BE DONE?

*I save anything that catches my eye—a thought, something in the paper—I save everything because I can't make that spot decision and say, "I don't need this now" or "This will be of use."\**
—John Guare

You're eager to write a play and you have a general idea of structure. You've set aside time to work on your play. You've sharpened your pencils. You plugged in the computer. What's next? What process should one follow?

In the same way that there aren't laws that dictate the path a play must take, there are no commandments to direct the kind of process that should be followed. Each playwright will be guided by their own instincts.

There are, however, certain habits that one will want to cultivate, and they can be roughly slotted into two categories.

## HABITS OF PLACE

It will be important to maintain some sort of dedicated space where the play can take shape. That place can take many different forms. It can be as simple as an electronic file in your computer, or as old-fashioned as a file folder. It can be a dog-eared notebook, or a cluttered desktop.

---

\* Buzz McLaughlin, *The Playwright's Process: Learning the Craft from Today's Leading Dramatists* (New York: Back Stage Books, 1997), 64.

The space only serves as a kind of holding station; a repository for all the ideas that you may generate—some useful and others not. The point is you won't necessarily be able to detect the difference between the useful and the useless ideas initially, so you'll need some place where you can store them as they arrive.

At this stage you won't want to throw out anything, so the space should be able to accommodate your protean play as it grows and develops through different stages and drafts.

# HABITS OF PROCESS

It will be equally important that you develop a writing routine that works for you. If you're like every other writer, that will take some thinking.

Summoning a story can be a bit like conjuring a spirit. Everyone has their own particular rituals that they invoke. Some people find that a strict schedule suits them. They "go to work" at certain hours of the day, and the very act of sitting down and setting up creates an arena that allows them to channel their imagination.

Some writers require separation and feel that leaving their normal environment helps them to shed the other concerns of the day and focus entirely on the needs of character and story. Others feel that the struggle with story is so ongoing a process that you must carry your writing materials with you and be prepared to stop, drop, and write whenever you feel the necessity, at the dinner table, by the bed, or wherever. This carry-it-with-you approach can also be necessary if the rest of life won't let go. I recall speaking with one playwright who had written many of her best plays at the same time that she was raising a young family. She wryly observed that if she'd waited for the "right time" to work, she would have waited forever. Instead she decided that the rest of her life would just have to make room. In the morning she would plunk her notebook down beside the breakfast dishes and get after writing while the kids wolfed down their cereal.

Regardless of the obstacles that stand in the way of your work (and you can count on it that there will be many—the rule of thumb is that almost everything conspires to prevent you from writing), you should attempt to check in and develop your play daily. If you find that your work week has more days away from writing than days when you're productively engaged, you may want to readjust it.

So find the place where you can collect your work, and find the process that suits you—and you're ready to begin.

# FORMAT

Perhaps the first place to begin is by examining how words are laid out on the pages of a play.

In general, the public is most familiar with the format utilized by prose. This format employs a pattern of writing organized into sentences and paragraphs on a page. Each sentence is further separated into units of meaning by commas, semicolons, colons, and periods. Here, as in most things, form follows function.

At one time there were no paragraphs, nor commas, nor any other kind of punctuation. When monks first handwrote biblical passages on parchment, it was common that the work would be inscribed so that it simply flowed across the page without hesitation, punctuation, or separation. It was thought that by writing in this fashion it would cause the reader to struggle harder and work their way toward the intended meaning of the work.

Of course, not everyone found their way to the intended meaning. Instead, people became confused by the sprawling, crawling mess of words. There were many mistakes and errors made in meaning, and eventually a precise grammatical structure evolved. That structure allows you and me to read text today and decipher, with some precision, what the writer meant.

Plays also have evolved a particular written format, and that structure is guided by the intention of the document. Traditionally, a playscript is not meant to be read, but to be performed. The text is simply a blueprint that allows all the parties involved to extract character and plot from the page and erect a meaningful production.

For this reason playwriting text is laid out on the page differently from prose.

# THE TITLE PAGE

The first page is the title page. It consists of the title of the play, written in upper case. Your name appears below it in title case (mixed upper and lower). This is followed by contact information. You may add the copyright symbol and date it, if you choose. Remember, though, simply by writing the script you automatically hold copyright. (An inexpensive way to establish and date copyright is to send it to yourself by registered mail and keep it in your files unopened.)

A title page looks like this:

TITLE OF PLAY
by
Author

# THE CAST PAGE

The cast page provides the reader with a quick snapshot of the characters in your play. It includes a very brief description of those characters and an indication of the setting. These descriptions should evoke clear, concise images without attempting to be too proscriptive.

The cast page provides a director or producer with information that is essential for production. A director may have a budget for only three actors. If your play requires six, there's no point in them reading any further.

This is how these elements are laid out for my play, *Illegal Entry*:

CAST

Garland: A tough-looking, tough-talking, seventeen-year-old kid. Stocky in build.

Jim: Sixteen years old and tall for his age.

Stuart: The youngest of the three. Fifteen. Quiet and very reserved.

SETTING

The exterior and interior of a small, attached garage.

# THE SCRIPT ITSELF

As mentioned earlier, a playscript isn't really meant to be read. It's not that it can't be read—clearly it can—but that's not its purpose. In the hands of a director and with the resources of a talented designer and cast, the script holds the potential to be translated off the page into something more dynamic that the audience will understand on the stage. For this reason, a playscript requires a specific written format.

Character names are set apart from the rest of the text so that the actor who must find and read the lines will be able to do so easily in rehearsal.

Stage directions are isolated from the rest of the text so that directors and designers can easily determine what action takes place, and then create a set and lighting plot that will best accommodate the action.

There are a few formats that are followed most often.

Left aligned is most commonly used in publishing. This format shares some similarities to the format used by novels, and consequently works best for those who are likely to just read the script.

In this style, characters' names appear at the left margin in capital letters. Dialogue is indented. Stage directions begin at the left margin and run across the page, or are indented in the same manner as dialogue. If indented, they are placed in italics, or in brackets. Stage directions and dialogue are always separated by a line's space.

Centre aligned is the more generally used for performance and production purposes. The format is jarring to those accustomed to reading prose, but for the purposes of production it separates all the elements of the script out distinctly so that they can be quickly retrieved by the actor, the designer, or the director.

In this style, the characters' names are centre aligned and appear above dialogue and within the stage directions. Some people prefer to capitalize the names of the characters as they appear in the stage directions, but the names of characters preceding the dialogue are always capitalized and aligned at a 2.5" tab stop. Some people employ boldface as well to set the character names apart, but it's not essential.

Employ sentence case for the dialogue. It should be single-spaced and run margin to margin. Leave a blank line between the dialogue and the next character's name.

Stage directions will appear at the 3.25" tab stop and run to the right margin. Often they're placed in brackets or italicized to further distinguish them.

When there is ambiguity about how a line of dialogue may be interpreted, a parenthetical may be used to clarify things. Parentheticals may also be utilized for line-specific stage directions and these are placed within the dialogue itself, in parenthesis.

In general, stage directions make reference to the particular geography of the setting (i.e., *Garland walks to the workbench and sits*) but on the occasion that the stage itself is referred to, note that the stage has its own terminology for describing direction. Stage right (SR) and stage left (SL) provide side to side direction on stage, stage left being the side of the stage that would be left from the actor's perspective, if the actor was on stage facing the audience. These directions are all from the actor's perspective, because they are meant *for* the actor, of course. Upstage (US) refers to the rear of the stage and downstage (DS) refers to the area nearest the audience. (This dates back to a time when stages were tilted, or raked, to allow the audience to see actors better.)

So, text from *Illegal Entry* is set out like this:

**JIM**
You think there's any other, you know . . .

**GARLAND**
What?

JIM

Secret compartment kind'a things.


GARLAND

What are you talking about? There are no secret compartments
here, okay?


JIM

What's that?


*He flicks cigarette ashes in the direction of the cabinet.*


GARLAND

That's a *cabinet*.


JIM

Well?


GARLAND

Well what? It's not secret.


JIM

Why not?


GARLAND

It's right where you can see it. Can you see it?


JIM

Yea.


But it could also be laid out like this:

**GARLAND:** So, how's it secret?

*JIM points at the cabinet.*

**JIM:** It's got a lock on it and everything.

**GARLAND:** That doesn't make it *secret*.

**JIM:** You can't tell what's in it.*

If you find the process of indenting and spacing troublesome or find that it interferes with your creative process, there are any number of software packages on the market that can be purchased to help facilitate formatting.

Format is the most mechanical portion of your writing, and in many ways the least important. It's the container. You supply the content.

Still, for some people, the devotion they have for clean and correct formatting approaches religious fervour (and in screenwriting, format *is* a religion).

There's no point in alienating your readers—and potential producers— by printing your script in a manner that confuses or annoys. The very first impression received is that of the text on the page. If there are errors, or if the layout appears sloppy, imprecise, erratic, or unclear, readers may take that as a sign of a lack of professionalism, and that's all some will need to put the text aside forever.

Don't allow that to happen. Don't provide anyone with the slightest excuse to dismiss your writing. Get the format down and become comfortable with it.

---

* Clem Martini, *Illegal Entry* (Toronto: Playwrights Canada Press, 1999), 23.

# PUNCTUATION

Because the spoken word inhabits such a central place in a play, there are a number of specific punctuation concerns that arise in this form.

Plays attempt to replicate all the rhythms, intonations, and contradictions that occur when humans actually talk to one another. How does one indicate when a thoughtful pause occurs in a conversation, as opposed to an awkward pause? How can one indicate when characters interrupt one another, or talk overtop of one another, or carry on parallel conversations?

There are certain symbols that are universal.

A dash ( — ) at the end of sentence generally indicates an interrupted thought or phrase.

An ellipsis ( . . . ) at the end of a sentence generally indicates that a thought or phrase trails off, or is otherwise left incomplete.

Some playwrights use the term "pause" to indicate a significant moment of silence within a conversation. Harold Pinter, for instance, has made notable use of this in his works. His play *The Birthday Party* begins in this fashion:

**MEG:** Is that you, Petey?

*Pause.*

Petey, is that you?

*Pause.*

Petey?

**PETEY:** What?*

Other playwrights prefer to signify a significant silence as a "beat."

Perhaps the most challenging aspect of attempting to capture human dialogue truthfully is that annoying habit people have of speaking at precisely the same time. Sometimes playwrights simply throw up their hands in despair and indicate in parenthesis at the beginning of such a portion that the following dialogue should be performed in an overlapping fashion.

Sometimes overlapping dialogue is indicated by arranging the dialogue in parallel on the page, like this:

| GARLAND | STUART |
|---|---|
| I'd back you up. It's like self defence, you know? Self defence? They don't put guys in jail for that. Me. *Me*, and *I'd back you up*. I'd back you up, Stuart. | Who's ever listened to me?<br><br>He wakes up, he'll tell. He'll tell everybody everything. I'm not going back to prison. |

Some playwrights create a special shorthand to accommodate the kinds of conversations that will be held between their characters. Caryl Churchill's play *Top Girls* features several characters speaking at once. Consequently, the script is prefaced with a small glossary of specific signals by way of explanation. She embeds a forward slash ( / ) in the dialogue to indicate where another character interrupts. She also uses an asterisk ( * ) at the end of a passage of dialogue that is interrupted, and then at the beginning of another passage of dialogue to indicate that the speech follows on from the speech that was interrupted earlier.

---

* Harold Pinter, *The Birthday Party*, in *The Birthday Party and The Room: 2 Plays by Harold Pinter* (New York: Grove Press, 1961), 9.

# ACTS AND SCENES

Plays often possess an interior structure consisting of **"acts"**—an act being an extended unit of action within a play. A shorter play may be comprised of a single act, but longer plays often have their action divided into several. Generally speaking, acts are made up of intensifying sequences of action—that is, Act Two is more intense and involved than Act One, Act Three is more intense and involved than Act Two, and so on. At one time it was not uncommon for a play to be written in five acts, but this longer structure fell out of favour in the nineteenth century, and the three-act structure then became the norm. By the end of the twentieth century the more common structure had become the two-act structure.

Within each act there can be found an echo of the overall dramatic structure. Each act is characterized by rising action and possesses its own beginning, middle, and end. In all but the last act, there is generally a crisis of sufficient consequence to generate the action of the subsequent act.

In discussions of narrative, the three-act format is often used as a kind of paradigm, in that most plays can be said to possess a beginning establishing action that corresponds with the movement of Act One, an intensifying and complicating action that corresponds with Act Two, and a crisis, climax, and resolution that corresponds with Act Three.

A playwright should put considerable thought into how they employ acts within the play because these acts will have an enormous impact upon the evolution of the narrative. As well, it's worth considering that every time the audience rises to stretch their legs following the end of an act, a playwright must ensure that they have built a powerful enough incentive to draw them back to their seats for the beginning of the next act.

**Scenes** are smaller units of action within a play that are generally defined by a change of location, or a separation of time. Although it is uncommon for audiences to leave during scene breaks, the very act of changing location or shifting to another time requires energy and attention from the audience. A play with many, many scenes will challenge the attention of the audience, tax their energy, and may prove too disorienting. There is an economic consideration as well, if the scenes require fresh locations. Each new location involves an expense. Write too many locations into your play and you may make it too expensive to produce.

# FULL-LENGTH PLAY VS. ONE-ACT

The most common forms to enjoy production on today's stages are one- and two-act plays.

Two-act plays are often referred to as "full-length" because their running time extends the full-length of what is commonly perceived to be a standard evening's entertainment, or about two to two-and-a-half hours.

It is uncommon to see a one-act play with a running time of more than sixty minutes. (Although not unheard of, and there have been a growing number of full-length one-act plays written over the past few decades.)

It is primarily two-act plays that are found on the stages of the commercial theatre. Within the time permitted by this form it is possible to convey fairly complicated, layered narratives.

Although a collection of one-act plays may on occasion be assembled for an evening's entertainment in the commercial theatre, one-acts tend to be produced primarily within universities, colleges, and at Fringe events. The shorter running time of the one-act is unforgiving, and, like the short story, its spiritual cousin, it best affords a direct, clean, clear narrative.

# SO, WHERE DO IDEAS
# COME FROM?

I think more than any other, this question is asked of playwrights. (With a close second being, "Can you really make a living as a playwright?") It's as though it was imagined that talented playwrights travelled to a special place—a place where other less-talented playwrights or people who can't write plays at all are forbidden to visit—to get their good ideas.

Let's be clear. There *is* no special place.

Some playwrights maintain writing journals as a way of generating ideas. They record their daily observations. They collect and assemble recollections and overheard snippets of dialogue. Bit by bit, within these journals, a story evolves or a character takes shape.

Other playwrights maintain meticulous files. Events from the Internet, news clippings, photos, and memorabilia of all sorts end up in these files and provide them with a rich source of material to draw upon.

Still others develop ideas by writing in character. They start from a single character's voice, slowly burrowing in, gradually cultivating this mysterious individual's voice on the page until they know precisely what he or she wants.

For some, a situation is essential, something that integrates the necessary qualities of desire and conflict and imbalance, and so they pay special attention to those occasions when conflict arises. Political turmoil, social unrest, and controversy provide them with inspiration.

For me, the moment I am able to clearly isolate a struggle that is associated with a specific and particular character, I feel I am well on my way. I have confidence that everything will unfold from the deeper understanding of that struggle and that individual. I keep gnawing at the situation until I know who else is involved, and how much is at stake. I use the energy locked in that struggle as my initial impulse, and then move out from there, examining the nature of the struggle and its consequences.

There are a few exercises provided near the end of this book that suggest other strategies for tapping into ideas—but the general rule is if you truly and fully engage in your own life, ideas generally appear. They arrive unbidden from observations of the world, from recollections of the past, from the interior world of imagination and invention. But above all, stories arise out of attentiveness. Attentiveness to the ordinary, the small, the quiet, and the everyday, as well as the extraordinary, loud, and singular.

One cultivates whatever unique process it is that allows you to grasp and hang on to the stories rolling past, through, and around you every moment of every day. You don't have to find them. You don't have to fetch them. Just open your eyes.

And don't block.

# WRITER'S BLOCK

Which brings us to that excellent term "writer's block"—excellent because it is so accurate. It implies that something has the ability to stop or block ideas from emerging—and the surprising thing is that the "thing" doing the blocking is the writer.

During the years I spent working with an improvisational company there was a good deal of discussion about blocking. It was an interesting time, that. On a good day you were able to conjure situations and characters out of thin air, like a magician. Audiences would often approach after a show and ask if there wasn't really a hidden text somewhere that we had quickly memorized.

Well, there was no undisclosed text. There was simply a technique that worked, and that technique could be distilled into the following observations. Since it was necessary to generate a story instantly, you couldn't afford to *wait* for a good idea to occur. Instead, you had to accept ordinary ideas as they occurred, and then trust that with attention and energy those ideas could become good.

The single biggest tenet we followed was not to "block." A "block" was any time you obstructed, denied, or killed an idea, and as an improviser you quickly came to a realization that most people spend their whole lives doing just that. Most ideas—when they initially appear—seem too crazy, too intimate, too profane, too threatening to embrace.

Bad improvisers spend their time on stage desperately searching for clever ideas that they pray will save them. They systematically crush ninety percent of the ideas that arise because the ideas don't, at first glance, look very promising. If they happen to be on stage with a fellow improviser, they'll often try to win approval from the audience by comically killing their partners' ideas as well. That gets old pretty quick, because you can just about hear the seconds skidding by when nothing is happening on stage—and of course, nothing, absolutely nothing can happen if ideas aren't accepted and developed quickly.

What is writing, but improvising for the page? What is "writer's block" but a denial of creative impulse? Ideas are there, right next to you. You don't have to go far. You just have to make sure that you don't terminate them before they have a chance to mature. And if you stop to think about it, there are many great plays out there that are profane (*Oedipus Rex*, after all, features incest; *Cat on a Hot Tin Roof* spends its time trying to get Brick into bed; *Equus* explores the sexual/religious relationship between a stable boy and the horses) or violent (*Macbeth*, *Medea*, and *Hamlet* all feature a pretty high body count).

In *Impro*, his work on improvisation, Keith Johnstone sums it up nicely: "In life, most of us are highly skilled at suppressing action. All the improvisation teacher has to do is reverse this skill and he creates very 'gifted' improvisers. Bad improvisers block action, often with a high degree of skill. Good improvisers develop action . . ."[*]

---

[*]  Keith Johnstone, *Impro: Improvisation and the Theatre* (London: Methuen, 1983), 95.

# WRITE WHAT YOU KNOW

You stare at a blank piece of paper, and ask, "What am I going to write?" Unless you have been raised on the moon, at one point or another you will have heard someone advise, "Write what you know."

And after all, what's the option—to write what you *don't* know? It's an awful trial listening to someone in a conversation striving mightily to bluff their way through a topic they have zero knowledge of, or background in.

It is the responsibility of the playwright to know what they are talking about. But when one talks about writing "what you know," it doesn't necessarily mean that you should write only delicate, realistic pieces inspired by your tortured upbringing (although there are a remarkable number of writers who have created famous works doing just that). Rather, it is about writing from a place of authority. What have you observed closely? What have you thought about habitually? What have you dreamt about repeatedly? What are you passionately, keenly interested in? If you want to write about something and don't feel confident of your knowledge, it's not absolutely essential that you be an expert at first. But you have to be prepared to perform the necessary work that will take you to a place of expertise. After all, eventually you will be responsible for inventing and shaping characters who are completely authentic seeming.

You are compelled to gain some knowledge of virtually everything in a play: the setting, the background of the characters, the relationships, the secrets, the dialects, the way your characters walk, how they talk, what they eat, where they were born.

The lot. In a sense the very nature of playwriting necessitates that you become a multidisciplinarian—and the audience expects this from you. If you falter, if the audience catches you out, if they listen to the voice of a character and go, "That's not how they would talk," then they lose confidence in your entire creation.

This doesn't preclude you from writing about people, places, or situations other than the folks and situations you have yourself encountered or lived with. Imagining things *is*, after all, kind of the writer's job. But—and it's a big but—one of the principal reasons that individuals from a variety of different cultural and ethnic groups have objected to "outsiders" trying to chronicle their stories is because the outsiders have so often got it so spectacularly wrong. Examine some of the great villains of Victorian literature, or from the early thirties and forties, and you will encounter the worst kind of thin, shabbily sketched together ethnic, cultural, and sexual stereotypes.

The term "appropriation of voice" developed in reaction to so many writers pretending that they could write about people of whom they had only the vaguest understanding. If you wish to take on subject matter outside your understanding, you have a responsibility to do the necessary rigorous research.

Working from a place of authenticity will allow you to:

1. Create a set of circumstances that you have observed closely and understood well.

2. Develop a world that is complete in small and detailed ways. Work from an unconscious level.

3. Develop voices that are nuanced and complex.

You are most likely to be able to craft a story in a setting you are completely familiar with. You will know the rules. You'll know the jargon. You'll know the secrets, and the secrets behind the secrets. The story will take on a particular and specific life because the characters will feel like they have all that rich history and background fuelling them.

So, write what you know, or make the extra effort necessary to become better informed about what you wish to write. Your choice.

# DISCUSSING OUTLINES

Once you have connected with an idea, developing an outline isn't a bad way to proceed. The trouble is so many people loathe outlines. They're too confining, they complain. They don't allow for invention and discovery.

Well, maybe they don't, but let me ask you—would you walk into the wilderness without a map? Not readily. An outline *is* the map. It's a map you carry as you venture into the wilderness of your imagination. It *guides you*. It can't compel you. It does not control you. If you choose to stray from the path you initially selected, that's up to you. If you decide to stay longer, stray farther, or just chuck the whole darn map into the swamp and wander knee deep in murky water and snakes—again, up to you.

But . . . if you hike off into the wilderness without a sense of where you're going, there's a chance that you'll stagger about, get tired, get frustrated, get good and lost, and only your bleached bones will be found. That's exactly what happens, figuratively, to a number of writers when they decide to fly blind.

But, some argue, that's precisely the point. "I don't want to *know* where I'm going," they cry. "If I already *knew* where I was going, there would hardly be any point in going in the first place." It is by getting lost, they argue, that one discovers the uncharted. Using an outline simply ensures that you will go where you have already gone.

You see how it is? There's almost *nothing* that playwrights agree on. Just as playwriting isn't governed by rules, there are no rules that can really be applied to outlines. Every person ends up creating a method that works for them.

There are a few ways that individuals, depending upon their temperament, tend to go.

# THE COMPLETE OUTLINE

The complete outline contains a number of elements and requires a fair amount of organization and effort. This is the preferred method for those who would rather execute the majority of the difficult structural work right off the top.

The theory behind choosing this strategy is that if you have your story structure well in hand, it will free you to immerse yourself in the actual scene-by-scene creativity when you turn to the next stage, which is writing the script itself.

In this process, one tries to break down and unlock all the essential structural elements of the script. A complete outline, then, contains these ingredients:

## 1. *A Working Title*

You are always struggling to move to a place of greater definition, so even if it's only a working title, attempt to put a name to your play.

There are many different techniques that playwrights adopt to arrive at their titles. Some name their play after the protagonist of the story: *Othello, Mother Courage and Her Children, Zastrozzi, Galileo.* Some frame the action of the play within the title: *Death of a Salesman, The Trials of Brother Jero, Betrayal, Leaving Home.* Others find a significant icon, object, or image useful: *Buried Child, White Biting Dog, Rhinoceros.* And others still find extracting a line from the text, or another related text, can work, such as in the case of Edward Albee's *Who's Afraid of Virginia Woolf?*

Whatever process you employ, you should strive to put a title of some sort—even if it is only a temporary title—in place soon.

The title is one more thing that will help to keep the story anchored and focused. That working title can be changed later if a more appropriate one comes to mind—and of course that's true of everything in the outline. It's always possible to change.

## 2. A Cast List and Character Description

A character description is extremely useful. It should provide the essential background material of your characters. How old are they? What do they do? How are they related to one another in the narrative? What are their essential desires and through-lines in the story?

## 3. A Setting

Describe briefly where and when the play takes place. This will allow you to determine how many locations are absolutely necessary. Remember that each location requires time, energy, and expense.

## 4. A Story Synopsis

Describe in a paragraph or two what the play is about. This exercise allows you to crystallize the essential sweep of the story.

Drafting the synopsis often causes writers grief. How, they wonder, will they ever be able to accurately render their sprawling, complicated, emotionally rich story in one paragraph and do it justice? But that's precisely what makes the exercise so useful. By distilling the play into a paragraph for others you may very well isolate the most important elements for yourself.

And if you get good at this, it can only make your life easier. There are many, many folks out there who will want to read this condensed form of your story in the future. Many theatres prefer to receive a synopsis first when you pitch them a play, and only if the synopsis grabs them will they invite you to send your script. Likewise, granting agencies, publishers, film producers, and publicists all share a great fondness for the synopsis.

## 5. A Scene by Scene Breakdown of the Play

Each scene should be described in a paragraph or two, with emphasis on the significant actions and conflicts that occur. Where action and time plays continuously, the scenes are broken into sections according to either significant units of conflict, or, if you prefer, by entrance and exits of characters (referred to as French scenes).

# THE MINIMALIST'S APPROACH

This approach is essentially the same as the previous—except it's a fraction of the size. It utilizes only a very brief description of the characters, providing age, sex, and a one-line description of the setting. A single paragraph synopsis captures the essence of the plot.

This is followed by a one-page outline of the script that provides the arc of the play.

If the prior approach was the complete topographical map to guide you through the wilderness, this approach is more like the directions you'd draft on a matchbook cover. It provides direction—but you may have to stop the car from time to time to check out the landmarks.

# THE "FILL IN THE BLANKS" APPROACH

This approach is the complete opposite of the previously described approaches. It can be characterized a little like setting out to describe the interior of an unfamiliar, pitch dark room by entering each day, picking something up, feeling it carefully in your hands, and then returning to your desk to describe what you've found.

It may take you a while, but eventually, by proceeding carefully, you will grow to know that dark room quite well.

In this approach, the playwright is not so much trying to "create" an outline, as they are attempting to describe a structure that is already imagined to exist. As the writer becomes familiar with the shape and form of the narrative, they are able to slowly add to it, alter it, and edit it; and once they understand the essential layout of the land, they can set out to write their first draft.

Harold Pinter, in his Nobel Prize acceptance speech describes his process this way:

*. . . In the play that became* The Homecoming *I saw a man enter a stark room and ask his question of a younger man sitting on an ugly sofa reading a racing paper. I somehow suspected that A was a father and that B was his son, but I had no proof. This was however confirmed a short time later when B (later to become Lenny) says to A (later to become Max), "Dad, do you mind if I change the subject?" . . .*

Each venture into the dark room brings back another revelation, another piece of the puzzle.

# THE SYNTHESIS

This process borrows elements from several camps. In this version, a brief, formalized outline is developed—but rather than waiting for it to be absolutely completed, the writer simultaneously, and in parallel with that procedure, sets about drafting exploratory scenes.

This is the method I personally find most useful. It puts me in possession of a short, clear outline—eventually—while at the same time permitting me to make new discoveries in the yet to be defined and still very unformed wilderness of that imagined world. It allows me to return and apply these discoveries to the developing outline.

If I come across a new, previously unimagined conflict between two characters, I simply integrate the new information. Finally, I settle upon a complete outline that I am satisfied with, and most often I have developed portions of the text at the same time.

With these elements in hand, I proceed to a first draft.

---

* Harold Pinter, "Art, Truth and Politics," Nobel Prize, 2005, https://www.nobelprize.org/prizes/literature/2005/pinter/25621-harold-pinter-nobel-lecture-2005/.

# BACKSTORY—
# THE BEGINNING BEFORE
# THE BEGINNING

Every play has deep roots.

Story is constructed upon and only exists because of everything that happened prior. As the play slowly grows out from its base, it relies upon those roots for grounding, nourishment, and support.

To know what is truly at stake, to understand the relationships between characters, to comprehend the decisions that characters will make as the story advances, it is essential to have a thorough understanding of what has transpired before.

Sharon Pollock's play *Doc*, for example, examines the life of a doctor on Canada's East Coast. The play is largely determined by and requires a knowledge of the doctor's past.

Arthur Miller's *Death of Salesman* chronicles the life of Willy Loman, the rearing of his children Biff and Happy, and in a sense the lives of Willy's deceased father and uncle as well.

Bertolt Brecht's *Galileo* is built upon the relationship of the Catholic Church to the development of science, and *The Death of Marat* draws upon the turmoil of the French Revolution.

Some playwrights consider this chronicling of the past an essential part of their research, and before they begin to write the play they will construct a historical background for their characters. Out of history emerges incident. Out of incident emerges story. The more you discover about the relationships and situations prior to the play, the more the play itself emerges.

Others find that if they stay close to their characters as they surge into the future and pursue their objectives, the history will begin to materialize. If that is the particular process you use, you should be prepared to allow the story itself to modify as the history solidifies.

# RESEARCH

Before the set designer creates the sets, you have already envisioned them in your own mind. Before actors breathe life into the characters, you have already animated those characters in your own mind. Before any of these others may advance into the universe of your script, you must have ventured there first.

If that sounds like a lot of work, it is, and often it requires thorough research. People generally associate research with science- and technology-based efforts, but I encourage playwrights to perform an investigation before they begin writing as well.

That investigation may follow many different paths. The Internet and library are familiar sources, but one-on-one interviews can prove extremely valuable. Travelling to locations to take notes first-hand can offer up surprises, as can the review of old diaries and notebooks.

Some years back I wrote a play called *The Life History of the African Elephant*. It was inspired by a radio program I heard while sitting in my car. The program featured an interview with a zoo's elephant handler. I only had to listen a few minutes to understand that the handler had a completely different way of relating to his job.

To him it wasn't a duty, it was a calling. The elephants weren't a responsibility, they were family.

I decided that I'd better talk with him. I drove to the zoo, met with the handler, and after chatting for a short while we agreed to meet for a few more interviews. He invited me to the rear of the enclosure where I was introduced to the female elephants. They investigated me every bit as much as I investigated them. They extended their long trunks and sniffed me all over. I got a chance to pat them, to feel how rough and raspy their skins were, how solid their frames. At one point I attempted to shove aside the tip of an elephant's trunk as it crept toward my face. It was in that moment that I discovered just how surprisingly strong an elephant's trunk was. (You do *not* want to get into an arm-wrestling contest with an elephant's trunk. It's made up almost entirely of muscle and you will definitely lose!)

I learned so much in those sessions. I could not have even begun to write my play had I not first performed that initial research. The elephant trainer asked me something just before I left the last time.

"Do you know what the softest part of an elephant is to kiss?" he asked. I shook my head. The question had never occurred to me. "The eyelid," he said. "It's as soft as silk."

Research is full of such surprises. It poses questions that you never even would have thought to ask. In the end, anything that allows you to more completely envision your characters and the world your characters inhabit will prove enormously useful to you. Do your homework.

# PART FOUR
## BEGINNING

# BEGINNING TO BEGIN

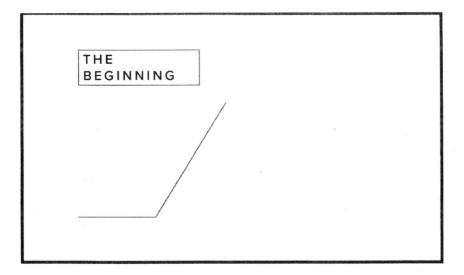

THE
BEGINNING

For purposes of clarity, "the beginning" of a play generally refers to the portion of the play that commences as soon as the curtain rises and extends to the point where the protagonist has encountered resistance and developed an initial strategy to overcome that resistance. Although the beginning of a play tends to be brief, there's no set amount of time or number of pages devoted to it. Some plays unfold gradually; others are abrupt and quick on the attack.

The beginning of a play resembles packing for a long and dangerous journey—there's a great deal of "provisioning." The individuals in the play are provided the tools necessary to proceed with their quests, and at the same time the audience is provided the tools it will require to comprehend the story.

The audience scrutinizes the play for meaning, and the "beginning" offers the audience the necessary clues to allow for that "decoding." The script introduces the principal characters. It firmly establishes the identity of the protagonist and the desire that motivates and defines the protagonist. It determines the action and the nature of the conflict. It defines the tone of the story.

If you haven't yet answered these questions in an outline, it will be essential that you do so fairly early on:

1. *Who?*

Before anything else, before you get caught up in questions of theme or idea or structure—ask yourself who is this about? A play, more than any other kind of story is about the "who." As discussed earlier, there's no other vehicle to carry the narrative forward but the actor, and so the focus is always, always, always on the "who."

2. *What?*

What desire drives this play? What precisely does your protagonist want? What is their goal or desire?

3. *Why?*

Why is this goal or desire important to your protagonist? Why must they act now? The answers to these questions will provide urgency and immediacy to your story. What will happen if your protagonist does not fulfill their desire?

4. *Where?*

Where does this story take place? What kind of arena will the action take place in? What is the importance of this location? Why couldn't it happen anywhere else?

5. *When?*

When does the story take place and over what time frame? A minute? A day? A lifetime?

6. *What's the Problem?*

What obstacles does your protagonist face? Who stands in the way?

7. *What's the Tone?*

Is this play a comedy? A drama? What's the nature of the conversation you will be sharing with the audience?

# CAUSE AND EFFECT

Plot isn't a random sequence of events. Rather, it's an interconnected series of events laid out in a pattern that is largely determined by **cause and effect**. Characters make decisions that have repercussions. Those repercussions, in turn, result in conflict, which results in further decisions, which have additional repercussions and result in additional—and most often more intense—conflict.

The audience concentrates upon these events, moment by moment, and struggles to determine how each scene is related to the previous scene, and what impact it will have on the subsequent scene.

You may have seen the game where a long series of dominos is laid out, sometimes in very elaborate looping patterns. The first standing domino is tipped and all the other standing dominos, one after another, topple as a result. Writing a play is something like that.

The snaking, twisting design is the plot, and each domino represents one unit of conflict. Each domino, as it drops, expends its energy and provides the impulse for the next domino and so on.

Here, then, is Shakespeare playing dominos.

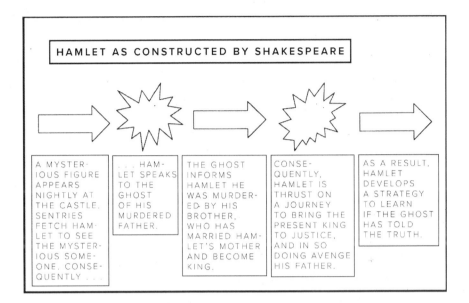

HAMLET AS CONSTRUCTED BY SHAKESPEARE

| A MYSTERIOUS FIGURE APPEARS NIGHTLY AT THE CASTLE. SENTRIES FETCH HAMLET TO SEE THE MYSTERIOUS SOMEONE. CONSEQUENTLY . . . | . . . HAMLET SPEAKS TO THE GHOST OF HIS MURDERED FATHER. | THE GHOST INFORMS HAMLET HE WAS MURDERED BY HIS BROTHER, WHO HAS MARRIED HAMLET'S MOTHER AND BECOME KING. | CONSEQUENTLY, HAMLET IS THRUST ON A JOURNEY TO BRING THE PRESENT KING TO JUSTICE, AND IN SO DOING AVENGE HIS FATHER. | AS A RESULT, HAMLET DEVELOPS A STRATEGY TO LEARN IF THE GHOST HAS TOLD THE TRUTH. |

This is what **cause and effect** can look like when executed effectively. Without the principle of **cause and effect,** things might look very differently.

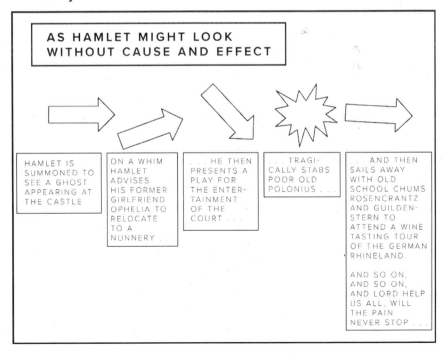

AS HAMLET MIGHT LOOK WITHOUT CAUSE AND EFFECT

| HAMLET IS SUMMONED TO SEE A GHOST APPEARING AT THE CASTLE | ON A WHIM HAMLET ADVISES HIS FORMER GIRLFRIEND OPHELIA TO RELOCATE TO A NUNNERY . . . | . . . HE THEN PRESENTS A PLAY FOR THE ENTERTAINMENT OF THE COURT . . . | . . . TRAGICALLY STABS POOR OLD POLONIUS . . . | . . . AND THEN SAILS AWAY WITH OLD SCHOOL CHUMS ROSENCRANTZ AND GUILDENSTERN TO ATTEND A WINE TASTING TOUR OF THE GERMAN RHINELAND. AND SO ON, AND SO ON, AND LORD HELP US ALL, WILL THE PAIN NEVER STOP . . . |

It is not so much the events themselves that are the story, but the arrangement of the events. Each event is not only a unit of narrative in and of itself, but it is connected to events both extending into the future and stretching into the past, and each event serves to activate the next.

# REMEMBER—YOU ARE NOT TRYING TO TELL EVERYTHING

Although, when you write a play, you are drawing upon an entire world, you are not attempting to mount that entire world on the stage.

The story of *Hamlet* details a very specific time in Hamlet's life. One can imagine that other things occurred in Hamlet's life. Maybe he had a very happy childhood and a number of rascally friends. Maybe he had a wild and reckless adolescence. Doesn't matter. The story of *Hamlet*, as related by Shakespeare, is short, deliberate, and very clearly defined.

Selection is, in many ways, a critical action of the playwright in this early stage of playwriting. The playwright selects the individual upon whom the story will rest. Likewise, it is up to the playwright to select a specific and particular time when change can occur. That specific and particular time may be one hour, one day, one century, or several critical moments in one lifetime—it's up to you.

But it is more than selecting a time, it is about being clear in your own mind about the unity of the piece. What is *it* and what is *it* all about?

# EXPOSITION

**Exposition** is information that is essential to the understanding of a play. Although **exposition** can occur anywhere in a play, the beginning is where the greatest amount is generally found. The beginning is, after all, the place where the audience is introduced to plot, character, and the world of your story.

But exposition is dangerous. Like cholesterol, which medical authorities inform us can be divided into a beneficial, handy kind that aids the body and a bad sort that clogs your arteries, there's effective **exposition** that can illuminate your play and ineffective **exposition** that can cripple your play, causing it to seize up, keel over, and die.

# . . . AND INEFFECTIVE EXPOSITION

The following scene reflects some of the symptoms of ineffective delivery of exposition.

> BILL *walks up the street with a package under his arm. He encounters his friendly, outgoing neighbour,* LEONA.

**BILL:** Hello, Leona, who is also my neighbour from two doors up the block, my confidante and supporter throughout my recent troubles. I hope that you have had a good day this sunny Friday the thirteenth of July, which is an unlucky date to be sure, and of which I am justly suspicious having had uncommonly bad luck myself on the past several Friday the thirteenths, what with the death of my dog, Snuffy the Second, the previous Friday the thirteenth of April, and my unexpected termination from the only job I ever loved at the zoo where I took care of the primates like they were my very own family, until that new, younger zoo director, who has a completely different and much more commercial and unfeeling vision of how a zoo should be operated, was hired, tragically, on Friday the thirteenth of November last. How well I remember that day!

This exposition is ineffective, not only because it suffers from run-on sentences, poor punctuation, and an unfortunate selection of names for pets, but because it tries so desperately to cram too much information into too short a space.

It's ineffective because it delivers information that the person who is being addressed can already be assumed to know. After all, one can assume that Leona already knows that she is Bill's neighbour and confidante. She certainly knows how many doors up the block she lives.

It's ineffective because it impedes rather than propels action. All that information may be useful to the story, but it hasn't left Bill much room to pursue any particular desire.

It's ineffective because it is so obviously relaying information for the benefit of the audience. Consequently, any illusion that Bill and Leona have lives independent of the writer or the audience is abandoned.

It's ineffective because it feels unnatural. Why would one person deliver so much information with so little reason?

So perhaps this example presents an extreme vision of how exposition can go awry—but it's not as extreme as you might think. There are many playwrights who have similarly resorted to staging bogus phone calls, or having letters read aloud in their plays to set up the scene, to provide essential background, or to establish an important plot point.

And it doesn't necessarily make things any less painful if **exposition** is shared between characters.

Let's return to Bill and Leona for a moment.

LEONA *walks with* BILL.

**LEONA:** I feel so sad about you losing your job at the zoo, Bill. It has literally wrenched at my heart and twisted my stomach into knots.

**BILL:** The nearly fifteen years I spent working with gorillas and gibbons were some of my happiest times, and of course now I have nothing to do but drink beer by the case, which is why I have all these empties clutched under my arm, to return to the bottle depot down the block.

**LEONA:** Bill, how worrisome it is to me that drinking has become such a crutch for you in this time of depression and anxiety. Primates were your life! But somehow you must retain your dignity—the positive thing to hold onto is that the gorillas will remember you because studies have shown that they have very highly developed cognitive skills, in addition to their remarkable hand-to-eye coordination. They would make excellent baseball players, if only uniforms were made to fit their unusual torso-to-hip body ratio, and if they didn't have to run the bases, because, as you know, their bipedal skills are not really adapted to quick locomotion over open terrain.

**BILL:** *(quietly, but with great intensity)* I love baseball as well.

Again, in addition to stilted dialogue and static, unfocused storytelling, this portion can lay claim to serious **exposition** issues. Some of the **exposition** is information the characters should already know, some of it is unnecessary to the story, some of it could be shown rather than spoken, and there's far too much of it all around.

Lean, efficient information delivery should be your goal. **Exposition** is delivered most seamlessly when it is released through conflict and action. There may be opportunities when a visual solution is more effective and elegant than burdening the characters with additional fact-filled, clunky dialogue, and, in any case, care should be taken not to try to unload too much information all at once.

# STUDIES IN BEGINNING

To understand how one begins a play, it may be worth examining how other playwrights have successfully begun theirs.

Something to consider as you begin to begin is that the theatre audience is put to work in a way that audiences of other narrative forms are not. The theatre audience—unlike the reader of a novel—actually has to travel somewhere to digest their narrative. It must sit still for a prolonged time. Unlike viewers of Netflix, the theatre audience cannot simply replay the scene. Unlike the viewer of a movie who can stretch their legs, leave the theatre to fetch popcorn, and have a friend provide a quick synopsis of the action when they return, the theatre audience must remain silent and watchful. Unlike readers of novels, they can't go back and capture something if they become confused. If the theatre audience misses something important, they may not be equipped to understand the subsequent moment or the next or the next.

To assist the theatre audience it's essential that the writing be clear—so the audience will not be confused. It is essential that the writing be spare and to the point—so that the theatre audience will not be forced to sit still forever. And it is essential that the writing be engaging—so that the audience will not be bored.

The following examples demonstrate how some playwrights have approached beginning their plays.

# STUDY ONE—
# *THE ADVENTURES OF A BLACK GIRL IN SEARCH OF GOD* BY DJANET SEARS

In her touching play *The Adventures of a Black Girl in Search of God*, Djanet Sears wastes no time. She immediately presents the audience with a gripping vision of a character in action. Her protagonist, Rainey, is seen racing down an empty road toward us. She's running as fast as she can down the centre line. Clutched in her arms, she carries a bundle.

> **RAINEY:** Oh God! Please, please, please God! Oh Jesus. Please. Oh God. Oh God. Oh God.*

Moments later Rainey lifts the bundle almost to her shoulders. The legs of a child involuntarily kick free from the bundle, then relax. The sound of a siren can be heard in the distance.

With an economy that is breathtaking we are introduced to both the protagonist of this story and an event that will change everything—the death of her child. This death thrusts Rainey into a painful search for meaning and God that will test her and consume her throughout the course of the play. The character, her quest, the tone, and style of the play are all clearly established in a matter of minutes.

Djanet Sears forgoes the slow and cautious approach of realism. Instead, she opts for a charged, stylized, theatrical distillation of time and place that ignites the beginning in a powerful sequence that:

1. With the death of her child, REVEALS THE PRECISE NATURE OF THE INCITING INCIDENT without providing any unnecessary details. More information will be provided later in the play as required.

---

* Djanet Sears, *The Adventures of a Black Girl in Search of God* (Toronto: Playwrights Canada Press, 2003), 5.

2. CLEARLY INTRODUCES THE PROTAGONIST of the story and sets her at the forefront of the play.

3. Establishes the precise NATURE OF THE QUEST AND CONFLICT.

4. ENGAGES THE EMOTIONS of the audience promptly.

5. INTRODUCES THE STYLE of the play immediately. From the spare set description to the use of chorus, the play is informing the audience from word one that this play is not realistic in tone or execution, that instead it will jump through time and place as the story requires.

# STUDY TWO—*HAMLET* BY WILLIAM SHAKESPEARE

The first scene of *Hamlet* is set in the castle late at night. We learn from the guards that a ghost who looks very much like the recently deceased king of Denmark has been appearing nightly, and seems to wish to deliver some kind of message. In the next scene we move to the room in the castle where Hamlet meets with the present king and his mother, the queen. The king and queen urge Hamlet to cheer up and get over his father's death. Hamlet has expressed his intention to leave Denmark and go to Wittenberg to continue his studies. The king urges him to stay. Hamlet agrees, but when the king and queen leave, we learn just how upset he is.

> **HAMLET:** O, that this too too solid flesh would melt
> Thaw, and resolve itself into dew!
> Or that the Everlasting had not fix'd
> His canon 'gainst self-slaughter! O, God! O God!
> How weary, stale, flat and unprofitable
> Seem to me all the uses of this world!

Hamlet is interrupted by the entrance of Horatio, who informs him of the continued haunting of the castle. Horatio urges Hamlet to come and view the spectre. In scene four, Hamlet sees the ghost, follows him, and in scene five, he receives important news from the ghost.

**GHOST:** I am thy father's spirit,
Doom'd for a certain term to walk the night.

The ghost informs Hamlet that he was murdered by his brother, the present king, and he urges Hamlet to avenge his death.

**GHOST:** O, horrible! O, horrible! Most horrible!
If thou hast nature in thee, bear it not;
Let not the royal bed of Denmark be
A couch for luxury and damned incest.

Within a brief time Shakespeare has:

1. CAPTURED THE INTEREST OF THE AUDIENCE with a mystery—the meaning of the appearance of a ghost. The theatricality of the ghost's materialization is cleverly used to draw the audience into the story. We are first told that a ghost has been haunting the castle, and then the spirit appears and beckons Hamlet and us into the very heart of the tale.

2. CLEARLY SET THE STORY in a kingdom that is obviously very troubled.

3. REVEALED THAT THE PROTAGONIST, Hamlet, is also a very troubled individual. That's good. Those troubles provide Hamlet with additional inner obstacles to struggle with.

4. THRUST HAMLET ON A MISSION to bring the king to justice and set the kingdom to rights.

5. ILLUMINATED THE OPPOSING FORCES that Hamlet will have to face. Not only will he be opposed by a person who is ruthless enough to murder his own brother, but this person has at his disposal all the force and power of the kingdom. On another level, Hamlet will be opposed by his mother, who he still cares for, so the opposition takes on a very personal dimension.

6. REVEALED THAT THE STAKES ARE ENORMOUS. The journey Hamlet will travel has stakes that are political, moral, familial, and extend even into the world of the supernatural.

Is there any wonder why the play is the most produced of Shakespeare's works?

# STUDY THREE—*THE GLASS MENAGERIE* BY TENNESSEE WILLIAMS

Tennessee Williams begins *The Glass Menagerie* by establishing a very uneasy balance within a family gripped by dysfunction. Amanda Wingfield struggles to survive in a decrepit apartment with her son, Tom, and her crippled daughter, Laura. Amanda dreams of getting her daughter married.

This balance is upset when a friend of Tom's arrives for dinner—the "gentleman caller" whom Amanda hopes will marry Laura. Here's how Tennessee Williams has Tom deal with this information:

**TOM:** The play is memory. Being a memory play, it is dimly lighted, it is sentimental, it is not realistic. In memory everything seems to happen to music. That explains the fiddle in the wings.

I am the narrator of the play, and also a character in it. The other characters are my mother, Amanda, my sister, Laura, and a gentleman caller who appears in the final scenes. He is the most realistic character in the play, being an emissary from a world of reality that we were somehow set apart from. But since I have a poet's weakness for symbols, I am using this character also as a symbol; he is the long-delayed but always expected something that we live for.*

---

* Tennessee Williams, *The Glass Menagerie* (New York: Random House, 1949) 23.

Williams forgoes realistic exposition, and instead plants Tom as the narrator of the story. This allows Williams to collapse time, set things up quickly, and move to the true catalyst—the entrance of the gentleman caller.

In each case, within a few pages the audience knows who the play is about, where the play is set, the tone and style of the play, and the nature of the journey. Hamlet knows where he must look to find his father's murderer, Rainey knows that she must search for God, and Tom has planted the audience's focused gaze squarely on Laura and the gentleman caller.

# COMMONLY MADE MISTAKES

Before we continue, let's stop and consider a few things. It's easy to jump the tracks when writing a play. The following represents a short, but hardly exclusive, list of some of the more common problems writers initially encounter.

## 1. The "I Laughed Till I Stopped" Approach

The play is envisioned as a series of jokes. Each scene becomes a sequence of not very funny puns, clever asides, and irritating *bon mots*. The writing is arch and the characters all make merry. The humour tends to have a kind of numbing sameness, regardless of the originating character. Nothing really happens. Nobody is genuinely altered. No event has any genuine impact. The story doesn't progress. The reader/audience laughs politely at first, but quickly becomes bored.

## 2. The "All the Characters Talk the Same" Approach

The characters' voices sound exactly the same and they are all interested in precisely the same things. Each character appears to have sprung from the same background and handles their difficulties in much the same way.

### 3. *Frantically Chasing Originality*

The writer, afraid that they will be discovered to be untalented, unintelligent, unfunny, perverse—whatever—moves to other more original sources. Frequently someone else's. Almost invariably when someone strives for "originality" they end up sounding remarkably like something being done somewhere by someone else. So, the "original" writer adopts the tone or attitude or style of the latest novel, stand-up comedian, television series, musician—whatever material seems to best represent an unconventional stance.

### 4. *Set-Up-Itis*

A condition in which the playwright spends a great deal of time setting something up and feels that during this time it isn't really necessary to develop character or commit to any genuine conflict. The playwright operates under the assumption that when the Big Moment arrives in their play, it will make everything worthwhile. *Then* the audience will see and understand.

Of course, every moment must be one that simultaneously develops character and story. Don't ever believe you can simply set things up and the audience will patiently await the outcome. They won't.

### 5. *Giving Gifts*

This has got to be the single most commonly made mistake. The playwright gives their characters gifts instead of making them work for what they need. A character wishes to admonish someone—and then proceeds to do so without effort or interruption. Another character wishes to reveal their long felt but deeply hidden love for someone—and then does so in the most heartfelt manner. Our real life experiences tell us that conversations with emotional content are dangerous territory and tricky to deliver, so this approach rings false. People lie every day, not because they are evil but because telling the truth can be so darn uncomfortable. Let your characters be aware of the terrible risk that accompanies telling the truth and allow that awareness to have impact upon how they speak. Above all, make your characters work to achieve their goals.

## 6. The "Monologue Will Make It All Better" Approach

When things are getting tough and the playwright is finding it difficult to develop the story they often come upon a surprising discovery. If they just insert a monologue, the character can talk about himself and—voila!—now the character has additional depth and complexity. Right?

Not so much. Instead, the play often becomes burdened with text that doesn't advance the story. The shape, tone, and rhythm of the narrative is marred as a consequence. Crushing boredom ensues.

## 7. The "Surprise Ending Will Make It All Better" Approach

A subset of **set-up-itis**. In this scenario, the writer bends the plot, destroys characters, defies probability, and insults the audience, knowing in their heart of hearts that all will be forgiven when the audience finally arrives at their very special, terribly unique ending.

Don't be fooled. The audience will not wait for the ending. They will not even wait for the middle. If the play is not engaging moment by moment, they will leave.

## 8. Aimless Conversation

It's easy to believe that you have written a play if you have pages and pages of conversation. After all—people are talking. Conversation is happening. Something must be going on.

Remember, however, that while formatted dialogue may bear a seductive resemblance to a play, a play is in fact directed, focused action, and dialogue is only one small part of that equation.

## 9. Going on a "Talk About"

**Talk about** is related to both **set-up-itis** and **aimless conversation**. In this scenario, however, the characters' conversations are hardly aimless. Instead, they discuss terribly interesting things and are often very witty. Some of the subjects discussed may be truly intriguing, intellectually stimulating, or philosophically engaging. In the best versions, the characters feel distinct and have their own voices. But nothing happens. The characters don't appear to have any particular goals, or if they do have goals, they seem content to simply discuss them. Often this is accompanied by the sense that the characters have reached an emotional plateau. They never really seem to change their emotional stance. Consequently, the play feels stuck.

## 10. *The Jellyfish*

The characters lack spine. Personality traits are established and then contradicted so many times that it is impossible to determine who those people really are. This is related to . . .

## 11. *Unlikely-Plot-Itis*

Characters are yoked to, and eventually broken by, the efforts of pulling an unlikely plot. Characters perform so many unjustified, incomprehensible turns and flips that eventually the audience stops believing in them, or the play, or anything really, except for the discomfort of the chairs, the itch at the base of their backs and the tick-tick-ticking of their watches as time drags slowly, ever so slowly, on.

## 12. *Good Housekeeping School of Theatre*

In this version it's possible to detect all the elements at work. The structure seems sound, the characters appear grounded, and there's conflict, a decent amount.

But only a decent amount—not too much. Too much would seem excessive. Too much would feel uncomfortable. It would make the characters sweat. It might make them cry, or shout and swear. It would make them do things they normally would never do.

Which, of course, is exactly what you want.

Remember, it takes a lot to make people change. It almost always takes more than they would comfortably choose to do, and you do your characters and your play a disservice if you allow them to remain comfortable and safe.

13. *Armouring Up*

The characters are volatile and say and do extraordinary things. Terrible things. Hurtful things. And although other characters say extraordinary things in return, nobody ever really gets damaged. The words just bounce off as though they were all wearing thick, protective flak jackets.

This doesn't reflect life accurately, and the audience can perceive that. The audience understands from common experience that even insignificant slights can cause enormous hurt feelings. Nor is it dramatically productive if your characters deflect. What does the audience care if a character fulminates and fumes, stomps and storms, if it doesn't *change* somebody in some way?

The audience *wants* characters to get hurt. They want to see them crushed, terrified, haunted, taunted, humiliated, and tormented—and then they want to see them struggle to recover.

That sounds morbid, and I suppose it's possible that the audience enjoys this kind of activity out of a prurient, vicarious pleasure, but I believe something else is at work. The audience is afforded the unique opportunity to examine how people can survive in conditions when struggle and conflict are pushed to their most extreme boundaries and then recover without actually experiencing the hurt and pain themselves.

That's the invaluable grace that theatre provides.

Don't cheat the audience, don't cheat your characters, and don't cheat yourself by allowing your characters to armour up.

# PART FIVE
## MIDDLE

# THE MIDDLE—
# RISING ACTION

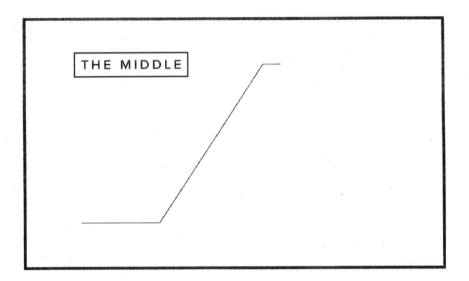

THE MIDDLE

*Many poets are skillful in constructing their complications, but their resolutions are poor. It is, however, necessary for both elements to be mastered.[*]*
—Aristotle

A play is born of trouble—and then things just get worse.

If the beginning of a play is characterized by introducing, establishing, and provisioning, the middle portion of a play is characterized by growth

---

[*] Golden and Hardison Jr., *Aristotle's Poetics*, 32.

and all the pain associated with growth. The characters must develop, the story must grow and mature, and the struggles themselves must escalate.

The middle portion of the play is the largest section of the narrative because it is where the greatest amount of the conflict is played out, and, generally speaking, it's where the heart of the play lies.

If, during the beginning of the play the conflict was initially defined and the protagonist provided a course of action, the middle is about examining how the protagonist now advances on that action and the obstacles they encounter in so doing.

It's a messy affair and for the characters it involves . . .

# CHOICES

There's no crystal ball to indicate what the future will hold—all we can do is stumble ahead and hope for the best. In the same manner, the characters of a play creep into the future blindfolded. Instead of following predetermined paths, they are presented with choices, the outcomes of which they (and the audience) are uncertain.

These **choices** are the mechanism through which the audience penetrates the characters. "What sort of person are they" the audience wonders—and then they observe a course of action that a character has selected, and they know.

In addition to permitting the audience an intimate understanding of the characters on stage, **choices** also serve on a more mechanical level to keep the audience engaged. Consider some of the choices that protagonists have been compelled to make.

CHOICE: Should I remain with my husband and live a safe but oppressed life, *or* leave him and lead a freer but much riskier existence?

*A Doll's House* by Henrik Ibsen.

CHOICE: Should I aid the person I've sworn on my honour to assist, and in doing so lose the only hope I have of connecting with the woman I love, *or* let him fail on his own, and perhaps gain an opportunity to woo her myself?

*Cyrano de Bergerac* by Edmond Rostand.

CHOICE: Should I continue to follow my passion and investigate the world but risk torture at the hands of the Inquisition, *or* should I give up my investigations, falsely admit that they were wrong, and risk losing my reason for living?

*Galileo* by Bertolt Brecht.

These choices are meant to be difficult. They are difficult for the audience as well. And as the audience empathically grapples with each choice, they are drawn deeper into the well of the narrative.

# EVERYONE IS A WRITER

Remember this, though. In a sense, the audience is busy writing their own play at the same time as they are viewing yours.

As they begin to grasp the journey your protagonist is travelling, they also begin to create their own imagined outcomes, and they are constantly checking this parallel composition against the script you have written.

If your play strays too far, or veers too suddenly from the expectations of your viewers, they may become confused, rebel, and disengage. On the other hand, the moment your audience anticipates future events with any regularity, then they may begin to leave—if not physically, then mentally.

There is a delicate tug of war between writer and audience embedded in this dynamic. Pull too little and the rope falls slack and becomes tangled. Pull too hard and the rope snaps.

# INTENSIFY AND COMPLICATE

Many novice playwrights place their characters in situations of jeopardy and turmoil, and still find their play flatlining and their audience bored.

Why?

Often it's a case of being confused about what constitutes "growth." It is not sufficient that a character be placed in one struggle after another. The struggles themselves need to proceed to an intensifying valuation and should transport the story to a place of greater involvement. It's not sufficient that your characters carefully develop solutions to the initial problem. The situation itself should respond and become more difficult and demanding.

If we return to the model of a laboratory for a moment, a play can be viewed as a kind of social laboratory. In this arena the audience learns certain things about a character by watching him solve a particular problem. But then what? In a scientific model, tests of a more general kind, once successfully completed, proceed to more rigorous tests with more exacting standards. This provides the examiner with new and more precise information by which to judge the truthfulness of a theorem. Likewise in drama, the audience wants to learn more, *needs* to learn more if they are to determine the accuracy of the protagonist's vision.

As a consequence, the flow of narrative surges from the general to the specific, from distance to intimacy, and from ignorance to understanding. Simply recycling equivalent units of conflict can achieve none of these things.

# A STUDY IN ESCALATION AND COMPLICATION

Let's examine Bertolt Brecht's *Mother Courage* for a moment to chronicle this process.

The play *Mother Courage* takes place between 1624 and 1636 during the Polish–Swedish War and the Thirty Years' War. Mother Courage, the cynical protagonist, treks from one place to another hauling her wagon of goods. She and her children manage a bit of a general store out of this wagon.

She hopes to profit from her sales to the troops fighting in the religious wars and aims to bring her family safely through the conflict, but the pressures upon her increase with each passing day. Though she attempts to keep a watchful eye upon her family, she loses her oldest son, Eilif, early in the play, when he is conscripted to fight. She struggles to keep the rest of her family intact, but Swiss Cheese, the second oldest son, is recruited to act as the paymaster for a Protestant regiment. When the Catholic forces overrun the troops, Swiss Cheese is captured, held prisoner, and brutally interrogated.

Suddenly Mother Courage is placed in a terrible situation. She must somehow find a way to retrieve her son before he is executed by the Catholic soldiers, and the only solution she can devise is to bribe them—but she can only raise sufficient funds for the bribe if she sells her cart. If she sells her cart, however, she will lose her only means to make a living and then she and her daughter may starve. In addition, Mother

Courage must take care not to reveal her relationship to Swiss Cheese, or the Catholic soldiers will take her prisoner as well.

So, she frantically negotiates for a fair price for the cart at the same time she tries to negotiate a fair price for the bribe. She struggles to retain enough money so that, should she be unable to recover the cart later, she will still have sufficient capital to start a new business.

In the end, she bargains too hard. The Catholic soldiers lose interest in the bribe and execute her son.

Others might allow the suffering to stop there, but Brecht has yet another turn of the screw in mind for Mother Courage.

The Catholic soldiers, intent upon learning where the paymaster's cash box has been hidden, decide to drag the body of Swiss Cheese to Mother Courage, to test her.

They reason that if she displays any emotion, it will prove she is related to him, and consequently may have knowledge of where the cash box has been concealed. They will then arrest and torture her.

So, she is confronted with the dead and battered body of her son—knowing full well that she is at least partially responsible for his death—and she is asked to identify him. Instead, she denies her own son and then watches as the soldiers heave his body into the flames like so much refuse.

Consider again the stages of escalation.

1. The Catholic soldiers overrun the Protestant's position. The result? Everyone associated with the Protestant troops, including Mother Courage and her children, are *placed in considerable jeopardy.*

2. Then, when the soldiers capture Swiss Cheese, things intensify. Suddenly, Mother Courage's family is placed in direct, immediate peril.

3. Mother Courage understands the military mind all too well, and on the basis of her knowledge she develops a strategy. She will bribe the soldiers and gain freedom for her son. *But, there's a complication.* The amount of money required is so great that it will place Mother Courage's business and livelihood at risk.

4. The negotiations falter. Recognizing the danger, Mother Courage urges the go-between to pay the full price. The soldiers, angered by the slow negotiations, become antsy. Her son's life hangs by a thread. *The situation intensifies* further as the deal threatens to unravel.

5. The soldiers torture and then kill Swiss Cheese, and then come to confront Mother Courage with the battered body. The emotional pain and turmoil this creates for Mother Courage is, of course, of a very high degree. But Mother Courage cannot reveal, must not reveal, any of that anguish because now her own life and that of her daughter are placed at risk.

The escalation and complication of this series of scenes is horrifically, but masterfully, orchestrated. Observe closely how Brecht exploits all these complicated feelings to raise the stakes ever higher. He doesn't attempt to portray Mother Courage as any better or any worse than what she really is. He acknowledges that she is a merchant. He recognizes that she wants to make a living and gain a profit. He invites us to watch how she agonizes over just how much she should pay to get her son back, how much she can *afford* to pay to get her son back, hoping to hang onto even a little money so that she can maintain her livelihood.

In lesser hands, Mother Courage would heroically ignore any complications, and pay any price to retrieve her beloved son. How much more imperfect, and therefore human, she becomes in the hands of Brecht.

Jason Sherman's *The League of Nathans* presents another contemporary study in escalation. The earlier portions of this play evoke young Nathan Abramowitz's childhood struggles as he studies for his bar mitzvah, and argues with his two close friends, Nathan Glass and Nathan Isaacs, "the League of Nathans" referred to in the title, about what it means to be a man.

Then one night, Nathan Abramowitz discovers that his comrade Nathan Glass has been implicated in the murder of a young Arab, and suddenly everything changes.

The stakes are raised enormously as Abramowitz is forced to re-examine what it means to be a man, what it means to be a friend, and where his true loyalties lie.

The pattern remains the same in each case. The path of the narrative climbs along a steep and tortuous route. It directs the protagonist continually upward through a series of increasingly demanding decisions, and finally conducts them to the very precipice.

# REVERSALS AND SETBACKS

The true measure of the risk involved in making decisions is gauged when a decision fails utterly. This event represents a thrilling moment in the narrative—and offers a tremendous opportunity to the writer.

When a character acts upon their desire and, rather than achieving the intended result, instead finds themselves in precisely the opposite position to what had been expected, this is called a reversal.

Reversals hold such great potential for tremendous dramatic impact because of the scale of the change involved between the expected and achieved results, and because the change arrives so unexpectedly.

In *The Seagull*, Anton Chekhov presents the audience with one of the more famous dramatic reversals. Treplev, a young artist, is interested in Nina, has expressed his love for her, and hopes that she will return his affection. He has recently staged a self-written play that failed badly. Unfortunately, Nina performed in the fiasco. Now Treplev feels she has lost interest in him as a result. He approaches her to try to gain her sympathy:

*TREPLEV comes in without a hat on, with a gun, and a dead seagull.*

**TREPLEV:** Are you all alone here?

**NINA:** Yes.

TREPLEV *lays the seagull at her feet.*

What does that mean?

**TREPLEV:** I was so mean as to kill this bird today. I lay it at your feet.

**NINA:** What is the matter with you?

*Picks up the bird and looks at it.*

**TREPLEV:** *(after a pause)* Soon I will kill myself in the same way.

**NINA:** You have so changed, I hardly know you.

**TREPLEV:** Yes, ever since the day when I hardly knew you. You have changed to me, your eyes are cold, you feel I'm in the way.

**NINA:** You have become irritable of late, you express yourself so incomprehensibly, in symbols. This bird is a symbol too, I suppose, but forgive me, I don't understand it. *(lays the seagull on the seat)* I'm too simple-minded to understand you.

**TREPLEV:** This began from the evening when my play came to grief so stupidly. Women never forgive failure. I have burnt it all; every scrap of it! If only you knew how miserable I am! Your growing cold to me is awful, incredible, as though I had woken up and found this lake had suddenly dried up or sunk into the earth. You have just said that you are too simple to understand me. What is there to understand? My play was not liked, you despise my inspiration, you already consider me commonplace, insignificant, like so many others . . .*

Hoping to gain the attention and affection of Nina, Treplev presents her with a dead seagull, and suggests that he is so despondent that he may apply the same treatment to himself. Will she feel sorry for him, he wonders.

---

* Anton Chekhov, *The Seagull* in *Nine Plays of Anton Chekhov*, (New York: Grosset & Dunlap, 1947), 30–31.

Instead of receiving sympathy, he is greeted with revulsion. Instead of achieving a reconciliation, Treplev finds that he has initiated an argument. Rather than getting what he wanted, he has created a situation that is much, much more emotionally charged and demanding.

Possibly the most celebrated reversal in dramatic literature occurs in Act III, Scene I of *Romeo and Juliet*. It happens precisely after Romeo has pronounced his love for Juliet and vowed to keep the peace between their feuding families. It's then that he and his relatives encounter their rival, Tybalt.

Romeo's only objective in that encounter is to deter violence. It is because of this that he places himself between the two hot bloods, his cousin Mercutio and their adversary Tybalt. It is as a result of his intervention, however, that Mercutio is distracted, and then fatally wounded. In fact, Tybalt stabs Mercutio right beneath Romeo's arms.

The full weight of this reversal is articulated in this emotionally charged exchange between Romeo and his dying kinsman.

**ROMEO:** Courage, man; the hurt cannot be much.  ·

**MERCUTIO:** No, 'tis not so deep as a well, nor so wide as a church door, but 'tis enough, 'twill serve. Ask for me tomorrow, and you shall find me a grave man. I am peppered, I warrant, for this world. A plague o' both your houses. Zounds, a dog, a rat, a mouse, a cat, to scratch a man to death! A braggart, a rogue, a villain, that fights by the book of arithmetic!— Why the devil came you between us? I was hurt under your arm.

**ROMEO:** I thought all for the best.

That is exactly the tragedy of this event. That in doing what he thought was "all for the best," Romeo achieves the exact opposite. After Mercutio dies, Tybalt returns and, in a rage, Romeo stabs and kills him.

His only desire had been to prevent conflict, but what has been the result? Suddenly Romeo has inadvertently caused the death of a beloved cousin.

Suddenly, rather than ingratiating himself with Juliet's family, he has murdered her beloved kinsman.

Suddenly Romeo is a criminal before the state.

Suddenly the union between Romeo and Juliet is placed in extreme jeopardy.

All these complicating circumstances serve to increase tension, lead to even greater complexity, and consequently even more difficult choices.

The ingredient least understood about the reversal is the element of abandon that it injects into the narrative mix. If characters can plan, plot, and apply themselves with the greatest diligence to a problem and still arrive at such calamitous results, then, the audience intuitively understands, anything at all can happen. The future is rendered truly uncertain, and the audience is compelled to follow events that much more carefully.

# DISTILLATION

All of writing, all of art, involves distillation.

The idea of distillation can perhaps best be understood through the judicious use of a really terrible simile. A play is like a freeze-dried meal.

In a play the *whole world* is presented—but only a very few elements are actually included. The imagination of the audience—like water in the previous completely forced and unnatural parallel—permits these elements to fuse and become an organic whole.

From the very first stick figures we draw as children, we perform incredibly audacious acts of distillation.

For instance . . .

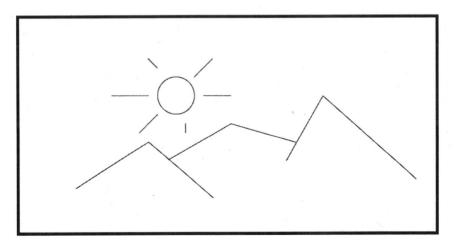

. . . a few quick, crudely drawn lines—something highly abstract when viewed objectively—become, through the reconstitutionary powers of an observer's imagination, symbolic of something much larger.

Shakespeare uses words to describe just such a process at the beginning of *Henry V* when he asks us to imagine "this wooden O."

> O for a Muse of fire, that would ascend
> The brightest heaven of invention,
> A kingdom for a stage, princes to act,
> And monarchs to behold the swelling scene!
> Then should the warlike Harry, like himself,
> Assume the port of Mars; and at his heels,
> Leash'd in like hounds, should famine, sword, and fire,
> Crouch for employment. But pardon, gentles all,
> The flat unraised spirits that hath dar'd
> On this unworthy scaffold to bring forth
> So great an object. Can this cockpit hold
> The vasty fields of France? Or may we cram
> Within this wooden O the very casques
> That did affright the air at Agincourt?
> O, pardon! since a crooked figure may
> Attest in little place a million;
> And let us, ciphers to this great accompt,
> On your imaginary forces work.
> Suppose within the girdle of these walls
> Are now confin'd two mighty monarchies,
> Whose high upreared and abutting fronts
> The perilous narrow ocean parts asunder.
> Piece out our imperfections with your thoughts:
> Into a thousand parts divide one man,
> And make imaginary puissance;
> Think, when we talk of horses, that you see them
> Printing their proud hoofs i' th' receiving earth;
> For 'tis your thoughts that now must deck our kings,
> Carry them here and there, jumping o'er times,
> Turning th' accomplishment of many years
> Into an hour-glass; for the which supply,

Admit me Chorus to this history;
Who prologue-like, your humble patience pray
Gently to hear, kindly to judge, our play.

This monologue not only *is* an act of distillation, but deftly *invokes* the act of distillation. When Shakespeare proposes to " . . . let us, ciphers to this great accompt, / On your imaginary forces work. / Suppose within the girdle of these walls / Are now confined two mighty monarchies . . . " he is *precisely* describing this process of distillation and reconstitution.

Life is disorderly. Life sprawls and spreads and wanders. The playwright's job is to isolate and carefully select certain particular atoms of meaning from across time and space. They then constitute these points within a precise structure so that when the audience summons heat and imagination, the points fuse and become, for them, in that time, emblematic of that portion of life.

# PARALLEL STRUCTURES

While plays are traditionally centred upon a single core of desire, there had already evolved among the ancient Greeks a more complicated construction involving simultaneously developed **parallel** plots.

In this structure there might be two or more plots embedded within a single narrative. These parallel stories are welded together by time, place, circumstance, or theme and serve in some manner to illuminate one another.

The Romans loved these more complex forms and modified them. Plautus, for instance, in his adaptation of *The Menaechmi*, shortened the prologue and provided room for additional comedy among the minor characters. The stories featured twin brothers separated during a business trip. Plautus snapped back and forth between the two brothers, developed each plot vigorously, and drew them together tidily in conclusion.

Shakespeare relished the notion that several plots could revolve around one another and employed the device in both his tragic and comic works (utilizing *The Menaechmi* once again, incidentally, as his model for *The Comedy of Errors*).

*A Midsummer Night's Dream* is one fine example of a central theme being explored through several interwoven plots. *Othello* is another in a more tragic vein.

This practice of developing multiple plots simultaneously has become a staple of television dramatic series, and contemporary theatrical works often make use of it as well. Brad Fraser's play *Unidentified Human Remains and the True Nature of Love* (later known as *Love and Human Remains*) juggles several plots, the principal being the relationship between David and Bernie. A secondary plot explores the relationship between Jerri and Candy, and an investigation of a series of gruesome murders locks the whole structure in place.

*Dry Lips Oughta Move to Kapuskasing* by Tomson Highway carefully blends multiple plots at the Wasyachigan Hill Indian Reserve, including the reconciliation of Zachary and Hera, the investigation of a tragedy that happened years ago, and the establishment of the Wasy Wailerettes, a female hockey team within a women's hockey league.

Each separate story provides characters and context for the others. Each separate story ascends along a line of rising action.

# POSING QUESTIONS

There's another way of viewing plays, and that's as a kind of Socratic exercise.

Socrates was a Greek philosopher and teacher who lived from 469 to 399 BCE, and was famous for asking questions of his students as a mechanism to instruct and develop deeper thinking. In playwriting, each story may also be represented as a series of questions first posed, then answered.

The beginning of the play defines the central dramatic question. It may be something as simple as, "Will Romeo and Juliet be able to sustain a romantic relationship in the face of the sustained disapproval of their families?" or it may be something as abstract as whether Godot—whoever Godot is—will or will not arrive, and whether there is any point in waiting?

Generally, the answer to this question posed at the beginning of the play is only answered at the conclusion—in a sense the play is the answer—but other questions arise out of this first question, and continue to arise each and every scene. Will Willy Loman succeed in convincing his boss's son to give him a raise? Will he and his sons come to a new understanding of one another? Can Willy face his past failures and learn from them in time to salvage his life?

It's hard to overemphasize the power this mechanism has to engage an audience. If the questions are sufficiently provoking, then the audience is compelled first to struggle to answer the questions themselves, then to probe ahead to the conclusion of the text to discover what answer will be revealed.

# PART SIX
## THE END

# THE END—RESOLUTION

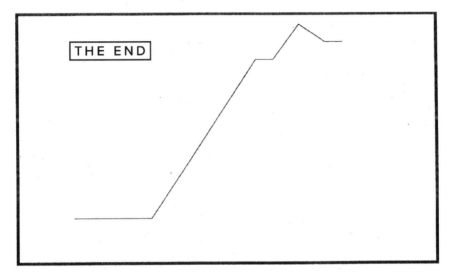

Finished, it's finished, nearly finished, it must be nearly finished.*
—Samuel Beckett, *Endgame*

The bad end unhappily, the good unluckily. That is what tragedy means.**
—Tom Stoppard

I never know when to end a play. I'd just as soon not end anything. But
you have to stop at some point, just to let people out of the theatre. I don't
like endings and I have a hard time with them . . . A resolution isn't an
ending; it's a strangulation.***
—Sam Shepard

---

* Samuel Beckett, *Endgame* (New York: Grove Press, 1958), 1.

** Tom Stoppard, "The Bad End Unhappily," American Association of Community
Theatre, https://aact.org/bad-end-unhappily-goo.

*** Cole, *Playwrights in Rehearsal*, 25.

In one sense the ending of a play is a very simple thing. Once you know what your **protagonist** wants, it follows that once they have either got what they wanted, or it's been determined that they will not get what they wanted, the play is over.

On the other hand, anyone who has ever written a play knows that crafting a satisfying ending is anything but simple.

If one considers the moment of **crisis**, one can see that this crucial event marks the beginning of the end of the **protagonist's** struggles. At this point the situation has developed in such a way that all other feasible strategies have been tried and exhausted.

If that is true—if there are, in fact, no other possible solutions—then once the final attempt has been made and is either successful, or not, the ending must be very close at hand. The climax marks that ultimate moment when desire has at last run its course. If desire is the ink that the playwright dips their pen into, at this point the well runs dry.

There are several things to consider as you construct the end of your play.

# ENSURE THAT THE CONFLICT LIES BETWEEN THE PRINCIPAL FORCES

The **protagonist** must challenge the principal force of antagonism.

Sometimes, it feels safer, easier, more convenient to arrange a confrontation with a lesser, more accessible force. Sometimes it seems almost impossible to design for the **protagonist** to meet and deal with the most daunting obstacle. Nonetheless, almost nothing else will fit the bill.

If, in the fairy tale "Jack and the Beanstalk," Jack were to climb the beanstalk, approach the castle, discover the monstrous giant, and then upon assessing the incredible size, terrible ferocity, and unmatched strength of the giant, suddenly reconsider things and slink back down the beanstalk to wrestle the scrawny individual who sold him the magic beans, the story would be diminished, as would our understanding of Jack.

There are other sundry foes that Macbeth meets as he pursues his goal of supremacy, but eventually he must confront his Macduff, just as

Antigone must confront her Creon, and Blanche her Stanley, and really there is no substitute. Once you've introduced the giant, there's no going back to the bean salesman.

# UNDERSTAND WHAT HAS CHANGED . . .

The resolution following the climax receives less attention than other structural elements, but it is at this point that the play is truly brought together.

When one finally arrives at the conclusion of *Oedipus Rex*, there are a number of dramatic events that can steal focus. One should remember, however, that although Oedipus is blinded and exiled, and although his mother and his wife have expired, society has at last been purged and cleansed. A kind of rough justice has been dispensed and life can carry on.

Viewed this way, the resolution isn't an afterthought that can be ignored or forgotten. It's *the* thought. It provides the audience with an opportunity to fully grasp the restorative impact of this **protagonist's** struggle.

# . . . AND WHO HAS CHANGED

There's no rule that says everyone in a play must change, but it's unlikely that the **protagonist** will be the only character altered. At the end of *Death of Salesman*, it's clear that Willy's struggle has concluded, but the play lingers to demonstrate how the others in the family have adjusted. At the end of *The Birthday Party*, Stanley is ominously hustled out by the thuggish Goldberg and McCann, but it's significant that the lights remain up long enough to reveal Petey abandoning him. This, the play is saying, is what the world looks like now.

In the end, the **protagonist** is a kind of projectile fired from the barrel of a gun. The audience has no way of understanding if the bullet has hit its mark unless there is an opportunity to closely examine the point of contact.

# IS RISING ACTION NECESSARILY A STEEP AND CONTINUOUS MOVEMENT?

No. The action of a play should develop, complicate, and intensify as it progresses, but it's unlikely, and not even particularly desirable, that it move forward in one smooth, uniform line.

The more likely progression is for the play to increase tension in increments, separated by moments of relaxation. This more accurately reflects life, where you hardly ever find a "uniform" anything. In addition, it's difficult for audiences to sustain tension over long periods, and they welcome a release before building to a new point of tension.

# BUT IS IT ABSOLUTELY NECESSARY FOR EVERY PLAY TO HAVE AN ENDING?

Every play *has* an ending. It's unavoidable. Even if you choose to end with an ellipsis . . . If that is the conclusion to your play, that is, by definition, your ending.

Not all plays have totally unambiguous endings, however, nor do all plays end neatly. *Waiting for Godot* ends ambiguously, as do many of Beckett's plays. Chekhov's play *The Cherry Orchard* ends somewhat ambiguously with the principal characters scattering; Fiers, the ancient servant, shuffling about, muttering about his ill health; and the sound of trees falling in the background.

The **desire** that drove the play should have run its course, and there should be a sense that something of significance has changed over the course of the play as a result, even if it is only the realization of your characters that, despite their best efforts, things have not changed.

# STUDIES IN ENDING

## STUDY ONE—*OEDIPUS REX* BY SOPHOCLES

Oedipus, the king of Thebes, attempts to rescue his people from a deadly plague. Apollo's oracle announces that all will be well once the murderer of the former king, Laius, has been found and exiled. Oedipus commits himself to finding the criminal.

This search for the truth culminates when Oedipus discovers that he himself is the murderer. At that point he is faced with his **crisis** and his ultimate **decision** about how to correct the situation. In the end, he chooses what he believes to be the only ethical solution. He blinds himself and retreats into a self-imposed exile.

The narrative moves by increments to a revelation of guilt and responsibility. As painful and horrific as the ending is, the old order is swept aside and a new order founded.

As an obscure side note, although this is certainly one of the best-known plays of all time, it's interesting to observe that Sophocles lost the ancient Greek Dionysia drama competition with this entry.

# STUDY TWO—*THE BIRTHDAY PARTY* BY HAROLD PINTER

The peace of a rooming house in Britain is shattered when two threatening strangers, Goldberg and McCann arrive. They seduce, intimidate, and entertain the residents of the rooming house, but eventually it becomes clear that they have some special issue with one individual, Stanley.

In this enigmatic struggle where the stakes are uncertain and the rules never clearly articulated, the question remains, who will prove victorious? During an evening birthday party celebration the **conflict** rises by stages through threats and muted intimidation to outright violence. When McCann finally ushers Stanley down from his room the following morning, Stanley's glasses are snapped and Stanley himself is barely able to speak.

The climax comes quickly. Despite the muted protestations of onlookers, Stanley is bundled up and roughly escorted out of the building to meet his mysterious fate. It is perfectly clear that opposing forces have met, contended, and McCann and Goldberg have triumphed. What the nature of that victory is remains ominously ambiguous.

# STUDY THREE—*FENCES* BY AUGUST WILSON

*Fences* chronicles the long development of Troy Maxson, a Black man struggling in a large urban American neighbourhood to raise his family. As he ages, he must face himself and his own failings and the question becomes whether he can survive. The climax of the play arises when his son, Cory, grows old enough and big enough to challenge his father. The confrontation escalates until at last Cory picks up a baseball bat and threatens to use it against Troy. In that moment, Troy, with all his age and imperfections, wrestles—and he is not only wrestling with his son, but with the mistakes he made in his life, with his failings as a husband and father, with his own violent past. Somehow he survives that confrontation, and somehow his son survives as well. Yet it's a remarkable triumph, because it is success without joy or even real satisfaction.

And the subsequent scene is an equally remarkable resolution that follows closely upon Troy's death, as we begin to comprehend the full legacy—both good and bad—that this proud, stubborn, complicated man has bequeathed to his family.

# REWRITING

You've finished the first draft of your play and you're pleased with yourself. There is, after all, not much that can compare with the tremendous satisfaction that accompanies this experience. It's more than an emotional or intellectual event—it is a genuine feast for the senses. There's the cool, pristine elegance of the document. The reassuring weight of the text as it rests on your lap. The soft and delicate thrum of the paper as you brush the crisp edges.

Many people believe that the initial burst of energy that goes into creating the first draft is the creative exercise and everything after that is a more mechanical function. Put another way, they believe that the right brain writes the first draft and then turns it over to the left brain for a spell-check.

Not so. It's often in **rewriting** that much, maybe even most, of the creative work really happens. **Rewriting** is the stage at which one can investigate character and story much more thoroughly, because at this point you know so much more than you did when you first began.

But... **rewriting** can be a tiring, wearing, soul-consuming exercise in futility if you don't go in with a plan. I have seen many writers approach their scripts knowing that *something* needed fixing, but not sure exactly what. They pick their scripts up. Read a bit. Agonize over how best to improve what they've written. Make a few tentative scribbles, and then place the script down in disgust and retire to the fridge for a snack. This kind of fitful rewriting can only lead to discouragement and weight gain.

Things proceed much easier if you break your rewriting into units.

# THE SIX STAGES OF REWRITING

1. INHALE AND . . . EXHALE. After an extended wrestle with your play, you may want to give yourself a breather. Take some time away from the text to develop some perspective.

2. READ AGAIN. After an adequate period of time has elapsed, sit down and have another look at the script from beginning to end and just make notes whenever your attention is drawn to a certain passage.

3. ASSESS. There are different areas that may need addressing. Is it the structure of the play that is requiring another look? Are there characters that need additional support?

4. PLAN. Draw up a list of those things you are best prepared to address. It may very well be that there are difficulties that you can't find your way to fix. That's okay. Proceed to the areas where you feel you can take action. Sometimes, once you have fixed the areas that most require repair, the next solutions will appear.

5. EXECUTE. It can be intimidating to remove text that you struggled and sweated to generate in the first place, but encourage yourself to be courageous. Implement your plans and see how things unfold.

6. EXPLORE. Where you still don't have a handle on what needs to be done, venture into the text and further investigate. If you're still frustrated it may be useful to have another person read the text and offer their opinion.

# READING THE PLAY ALOUD

Some of the simplest activities may have the most profound impact. Having a play read aloud is one such activity.

If you're a member of a writer's group, or a student in a writing class, gathering the necessary bodies for this event is relatively easy. If you're not connected to any formal group, simply round some friends up. Make the reading part of an entertaining, social evening with snacks and coffee offered after.

Once everyone has gathered, pass copies of your script around. Assign individuals their characters. Appoint someone to read the stage directions. Sit down. Get comfortable. Read. Now—and this is the hard part—listen. That's it.

Sounds pretty straightforward, doesn't it? But the payoff can be very rich. The moment you begin having your plays read aloud, everything changes. Until that moment you have only heard the characters through the filter of your own imagination, and that filter alters things. It makes every word sound reasonable and perfect. It allows your subconscious to run ahead and fill in all the holes and cracks in the rails before your train of consciousness chugs through.

Having others read your work invites the world to make sense of your words, and it, in turn, engages you in a discussion with that world.

There are immediate discoveries to be made as well as ones that pay longer term dividends. Do your characters all sound alike? You'll hear that for yourself and you'll watch as other people confirm it. Is the play funny? It's not unusual for writers to discover that the play they thought was dramatic and sober is in fact quite comic in places. And that may be a good thing.

There are questions you may wish to ask others and consider yourself following the reading:

Does each character have a distinct voice?

Do the characters sound authentic?

Are they true to themselves?

Where were you most engaged in the story?

Where did things seem to drag?

Are there plot inconsistencies?

Without turning the reading into an inquisition, gently urge your peers to reveal where things might have become confusing or troubling. These notes will be enormously helpful to you later as you revise.

# THE ART AND ETIQUETTE OF GIVING AND GETTING CRITIQUE

I know of writing classes that discourage praise in their critiques. The good stuff, according to this theory, will be universally recognized. The bad stuff must be sought out and destroyed.

That hasn't been my experience. My experience is that many people can't tell the good from the bad. For instance, there was a young woman in one of my classes. Whenever she received praise she would turn a bright red. Her lips would purse tight. One afternoon I asked her what the matter was. She responded by demanding why I was lying to her. She couldn't fathom or accept that she had created something entertaining. It's that way, or something like that, with many people.

The purpose of giving critique is to provide an artist with an objective opinion regarding the work. The artist has the right to accept or reject the critique, but if they are to be thoroughly informed, the critique should first paint a complete picture. Deliver the sweet with the bitter.

# ADVICE TO HELP DELIVER CRITIQUE

### 1. *Be Precise*

Telling someone that their writing is generally good or bad isn't very useful. Try to relate your comment to specific passages in the script.

### 2. *Questions are Good*

If you're confused by something in the text, you may want to phrase that commentary as a question. The question will allow the writer to perform their own investigation and work out an answer. It may allow them to identify an inconsistency and resolve it. Don't be surprised if they doesn't have an answer to your question right away, though. It might take days for them to consider the question fully.

### 3. *Don't Argue a Point*

The critique session isn't about you, and it's not about proving the essential truth or wisdom of your observation. Raise your question, make your point, and move on.

# ADVICE TO HELP SURVIVE CRITIQUE

### 1. *Don't Fuss*

If you're receiving critique, remember that the comments are delivered for *your* benefit. Snapping, muttering darkly, or flipping someone the finger is counterproductive and should be discouraged.

2. *Write it Down*

You may not understand some of the comments immediately. Full understanding might not occur until later that night, or later next week. Write the comments down so you won't forget them.

3. *The Things That go Wrong May be Just What You Need*

Someone laughs in the middle of your tragic monologue. That's not necessarily a bad thing. Worst case, this may inform you that you need to rewrite the monologue. Best case, it may say something about the tragicomic qualities of your piece—your audience may actually *welcome* the opportunity to laugh at this juncture.

4. *You Cannot Browbeat Your Group into Appreciating Your Play*

You can lecture your group for not getting this or that point of your play, you can point out the clever cultural references, but you cannot make them like it if they do not already. So don't try.

5. *Don't Feel You Have to Explain*

If there is some simple factual matter that can be clarified easily, by all means do so, but don't feel compelled to justify your play. If a passage was not understood in the reading, explaining it is not the answer anyway. And if someone has a question that you can't immediately answer, that's fine too. Perhaps the answer will occur to you later. Take the note and move on.

6. *The Loudest Opinion is not Necessarily Correct*

In every discussion there is someone who is louder, more opinionated, more insistent. This does not necessarily endow the individual with greater vision or understanding. Just nod and take notes.

# PART SEVEN
## CHARACTER, COMEDY, AND OTHER STRANGE ELEMENTS

# CHARACTER

Aristotle stated that a character should be "good, appropriate, conform to how they are in reality, and consistent." Since Aristotle's time at least, playwrights have continued to brood over what traits are most critical to the development of complete, compelling, and complicated characters.

Here are a few aspects to consider.

## THE PROTAGONIST

Saying only that the **protagonist** is someone who **desires** something is both too obvious and too general to be useful, because it goes far beyond that. The **protagonist** is someone who is *defined* by their desire. Macbeth is defined by his desire to become king. Antigone is defined by her desire for justice. Molière's Harpagon of *The Miser* is defined by his desire for money. Each character is defined by their **desire**—and, of course, their willingness to act upon that **desire** because simply wanting is never enough. The ability and willingness to act upon that **desire** is critical.

The **desire** should be of sufficient intensity that the protagonist is compelled to act upon it, and there should be a sense that there is the capacity within the protagonist to attain this goal. They may not ultimately achieve their goal, it may even at times appear unlikely, but it is important that the audience feel that there is at least the possibility.

# THE ANTAGONIST

Inasmuch as the **protagonist** is defined by their desire, the **antagonist** is defined by their opposition to the desire of the protagonist.

The additional interesting aspect of this dynamic is that while the **antagonist** is defined by the **protagonist**, the **antagonist** can in turn define the **protagonist** as well. Can anyone imagine Othello without Iago to fill his imagination with poison? Or Antigone without Creon to defy?

# NOT JUST PROTAGONISTS AND ANTAGONISTS

Drawn by the powerful force of the narrative, characters within a play tend to fracture and align along fault lines of conflict. They can generally be said to support or oppose the **desires** of the **protagonist**, or act as a catalyst to introduce some new force, energy, or impulse to the story.

Regardless of how they ally themselves, however, each character, minor or major, is moved by desire. They all want something, and they all have their own strategies. They all have their own stories as well, although the audience may never know the full extent of these side narratives.

It's been said that each character is, in their own secret heart, a hero—even the villain. In performing your rewrites it's useful to remember that.

# STATUS AND HIERARCHY

Common to humans of all cultures is the phenomenon of status. The term refers to behaviours that designate positions of power or deference within the framework of groups. Just as among wolves there are habits that assign the status of alpha and beta to certain wolves, there is conduct that consigns similar positions in most human groups.

This ascending order isn't rigid. It isn't fixed in time, and it's not fixed in space either. A person may hold higher status when they are a youngster in school, and then experience a drop in status as they mature. Likewise an individual may receive higher status at their workplace where they are considered a go-getter than what they are delegated by their soccer team, where their sports prowess may be less than average. But although this element of status may be ephemeral, almost every group imposes its own hierarchy.

Look at school kids at play in the schoolyard, and you'll see knots and clumps of youngsters relating in a specific way. Observe adults in a business meeting and you'll discover a similar phenomenon. Who has permission to speak most readily at social gatherings, and who dispenses that permission? Who defers to whom? All these matters are regulated by status.

When you develop characters it's important to understand that they never exist in isolation. They are, at least partially, defined and formed by the hierarchy that they exist, and struggle, within.

# CONTRAST

Place a white button on a white background. Now, shift that white button to a black background. How much more clearly does the button stand out against that second backdrop?

It's already been mentioned in passing that the differing natures of the **protagonist** and **antagonist** serve to establish clearer definition of their respective characters. In a similar way, it can be useful to position characters in such a way that the individuals they will spend the most time with on stage will provide contrast.

It's no accident, for instance, that Shakespeare pairs the sober, thoughtful, commanding Prospero with the quick, emotional sprite Ariel; or that he sends the status-conscious and deluded King Lear on a dangerous journey with his clear-sighted, quick-witted Fool. The world of the theatre is crowded with uncomfortable, awkward pairings.

Close proximity to someone of a different nature provides endless opportunity for **conflict**, but it also allows the audience to understand these characters in a new way. The distinctiveness of an individual's temperament is first noted by the audience when an individual performs an action, but it is then noted *again* in comparison as a result of the contrasting response of the attendant character.

# DISTINCT VOICE

Dialogue is another of the defining attributes of character. It should be possible to pick up a script, cover the names of the characters, read only the dialogue, and still have a pretty good notion of which character is speaking. If that isn't possible, ask yourself, "Do my characters possess their own distinct idiom and vernacular? Do they use sentence construction that is unique and particular?"

Review these examples of the spoken word as created by diverse playwrights and listen to the voices.

## STUDY ONE—*DRY LIPS OUGHTA MOVE TO KAPUSKASING* BY TOMSON HIGHWAY

Listen to Simon Starblanket speak in Tomson Highway's *Dry Lips Oughta Move to Kapuskasing* and compare his patterns of speech with those of the following characters.

**SIMON:** I stick my arms around this rock, this large black rock sticking out of the ground, right here on this spot. And then I hear this baby crying, from inside this rock. The baby is crying my name. As if I am somehow responsible for it being caught inside that rock. I can't move. My arms, my whole body, stuck to this. Then this . . . eagle . . . lands beside me, right over there. But this eagle has three faces, three women. And the eagle says to me: "The baby is crying, my grandchild is crying to hear the drum again."*

# STUDY TWO—*THE TRIALS OF BROTHER JERO* BY WOLE SOYINKA

**JERO:** *(gently)* Open your mind to God, brother. This is the tabernacle of Christ. Open your mind to God.

CHUME *is silent for a while, then bursts out suddenly.*

**CHUME:** Brother Jero, you must let me beat her!

**JERO:** What!

**CHUME:** *(desperately)* Just once, Prophet. Just once!

**JERO:** Brother Chume!

**CHUME:** Just once. Just one sound beating, and I swear not to ask again.

**JERO:** Apostate. Have I not told you the will of God in this matter?

**CHUME:** But I've got to beat her, Prophet. You must save me from madness.

---

* Tomson Highway, *Dry Lips Oughta Move to Kapuskasing* (Saskatoon: Fifth House Publishing, 1989), 44–45.

**JERO:** I will. But only if you obey me.

**CHUME:** In anything else, Prophet. But for this one, make you let me just beat 'am once.

**JERO:** Apostate!

**CHUME:** I no go beat 'am too hard. Jus' once, small small.

**JERO:** Traitor!

**CHUME:** Jus' this one time. I no' go ask again. Jus' do me this one favour, make a beat 'am today.*

# STUDY THREE—*TRAVESTIES* BY TOM STOPPARD

**CARR:** I learned three things in Zurich during the war. I wrote them down. Firstly, you're either a revolutionary or you're not, and if you're not you might as well be an artist as anything else. Secondly, if you can't be an artist, you might as well be a revolutionary . . . I forget the third thing.**

---

* Wole Soyinka, *Six Plays* (London: Methuen, 1984), 16–17.
** Tom Stoppard, *Travesties* (New York: Grove Press, 1975), 99.

# STUDY FOUR—4:48 PSYCHOSIS BY SARAH KANE

The protagonist remains unnamed in *4:48 Psychosis* by Sarah Kane:

A room of expressionless faces staring blankly at my pain, so devoid of meaning there must be evil intent.

Dr. This and Dr. That and Dr. Whatsit who's just passing and thought he'd pop in to take the piss as well. Burning in a hot tunnel of dismay, my humiliation complete as I shake without reason and stumble over words and have nothing to say about my "illness," which anyway amounts only to knowing there's no point in anything because I'm going to die.*

# STUDY FIVE—UNIDENTIFIED HUMAN REMAINS AND THE TRUE NATURE OF LOVE BY BRAD FRASER

*Lights rise on the apartment.* CANDY *is vacuuming and singing very loud.*

**CANDY:** Aphids on roses and nipples on kittens
Sleigh balls and snow balls and fat nylon mittens
Bright stupid packages tied up with string . . .

DAVID *enters from the bedroom. He has been wakened and is cranky.*

---

* Sarah Kane, *Sarah Kane: Complete Plays* (London: Methuen, 2001), 209.

**DAVID:** Candy.

**CANDY:** *(can't hear him)* These are a few of my favourite things.

**DAVID:** *(yells)* Candy!

*CANDY turns off the vacuum, very startled.*

**CANDY:** David?!

**DAVID:** It's nine o'clock in the morning for Christ's sake.

**CANDY:** I couldn't sleep. Tea's still hot. David, our floors are a mess.

*DAVID helps himself to tea.*

**DAVID:** We'll get to them.

**CANDY:** They're filthy.

**DAVID:** They're floors. People walk on them. It's unavoidable.

**CANDY:** They found another girl last night.*

---

\* Brad Fraser, *Unidentified Human Remains and the True Nature of Love* (Edmonton, NeWest Press, 1996), 58.

# STUDY SIX—*TOP GIRLS* BY CARYL CHURCHILL

**GRET:** There's lots of funny creatures round your feet, you don't like to look, like rats and lizards, and nasty things, a bum with a face, and fish with legs, and faces on things that don't have faces on. But they don't hurt, you just keep going. Well we'd had worse, you see, we'd had the Spanish. We'd all had family killed. My big son die on a wheel. Birds eat him. My baby, a soldier run her through with a sword. I'd had enough, I was mad . . .*

# STUDY SEVEN—*BARUNGIN* BY JACK DAVIS

**GRANNY DOLL:** Well, this Koolbardi—that's the magpie—and this Wahrdung—that's the crow—they was brothers, see. This was the time of kundum, dreams, see, and they was bi-i-ig strong men, and they both had beautiful whi-i-ite feathers. They used to fly around the lake and the water before the wetjala drained off the swamps, and they was moorditj hunters, but they was cruel jealous, jealous about who was the best lookin'.**

---

\* Caryl Churchill, *Top Girls* (London: Methuen, 1982), 29.
\*\* Jack Davis, *Barungin* (Sydney: Currency Press, 1988), 35.

# STUDY EIGHT—
# *THE CRACKWALKER*
# BY JUDITH THOMPSON

**THERESA:** Al he's coughin! Can't we get back some of that cough syrup?

**ALAN:** Listen stupid we're not usin any of that stuff I told ya! Didn't ya hear me or what? Listen. If he's coughin we'll just get that Vicks vapour rub that my old man used to use.

**THERESA:** That stuff smells too much!

**ALAN:** If it's good enough for my old man it's good enough for my baby, Therese. He used to put it all over his chest and his cough be gone the nex day. Here.

*He puts a whole jar of Vicks over the baby's body.*

**THERESA:** Al you putting too much!

**ALAN:** Don't tell me what to do! Shut up! I know what I'm doin I told ya the social worker said I was a great father! So shut up!

*He holds the baby up. It is glistening with the stuff.*

There. You're gonna be just fine now baby.

**THERESA:** Al you sure it ain't too much?*

---

\* Judith Thompson, *The Crackwalker* (Toronto: Playwrights Canada Press, 1980), 63–64.

**167**

# STUDY NINE—*BROTHEL #9* BY ANUSREE ROY

**JAMUNA:** Thirty-six hours my first time. Thirty-six. I be sitting there, Rekha, my first time. With my fat stomach. All by myself.

Second time. God have love for me. It is only for seven hours I am of pain. *(beat)* The first one was a girl. She was Barbal's father's baby. That was a long long time ago. I am new in business then. That was Barbal's father's way . . . that was his way of running business. Testing out the new girls by making them drown their babies.

I begged Ma Kali to be forgiving me.

*JAMUNA shows REKHA a scar on her chest.*

See this scar? I cut my chest and give my blood as offering for forgiveness. Begged her. Begged her with my own blood and made swear to never have another one.

*Pause.*

*(warmly)* Then come Salaudin. My janeman. Before he was police he used to sell telephone books door to door. When he hear I have fat stomach he say . . . drown.

I say to Salaudin, how? How I be drowning again, Salaudin. I cannot do this. How will these hands be holding that neck again after I promise to Ma Kali?*

After reading these contrasting passages, consider how each character selects words from a menu that reflects their own very unique background.

---

* Anusree Roy, *Brothel #9* (Toronto: Playwrights Canada Press, 2012), 68

Pay close attention to how each character arranges and prepares phrases.

"My big son die on a wheel. Birds eat him." "I no go beat 'am too hard. Jus' once, small small." "Begged her with my own blood and made swear to never have another one." The selection and configuration of these words represents a kind of DNA threading through each conversation containing information that defines each individual.

The characters are shaped by different cultures, moulded by different upbringings, instructed to communicate according to the conventions of their times. They may all inhabit earth, but they can truthfully be said to inhabit different worlds as well.

Stoppard's Henry Carr could no more hold a conversation with Judith Thompson's Alan than you could lift a telephone and speak with Charles Dickens's Little Nell. The language they use is one of the most important indicators of the divergent dimensions that these characters inhabit.

# THE INARTICULATE

Formalized language is only part of how humans express themselves. Within every individual's personal idiom there exists a whole assortment of inarticulate half phrasings, exultations, and grunts that reside outside proper grammar, and, to an extent, outside of language itself.

Listen carefully to intimate conversations and you will discover how much is characterized by groans, sighs, and other exhalations.

Just how extensive this inarticulate other language is can be indicated by the many, many mostly unsuccessful attempts that have been made to render these sounds into written form. The following awkward alphabetical combinations are just some of the manifestations of a variety of writers' various attempts to express this inexact code.

Pshaw. Tsk. Ugh. Agh. Argh. Ho. Ha. Hey. Mmm. Pfft. Yum. Hmm. Grrr. Uh. Whew. Phew. Ow. Ew. Eh. Ay. Oy. Shhh.

On the page they appear primitive and inadequate and cartoonish, but it's remarkable how dialogue that seems precious, overly articulate, and literary can become more natural seeming and curiously human when conventional language is stripped bare and supported by an inarticulate dialect of cries, gasps, hums, and sighs.

# SILENCE

It's interesting to think back to when Pinter's works were first produced how revolutionary his use of silence seemed. If you scan reviews of the time, a common refrain among them was how disconcerting and arresting those pauses were.

Beats and extended pauses are now merely considered an accurate reflection of how humans communicate, but silence remains a powerful tool of the dramatist.

Consider how it weighs down some conversations, and how it provides punctuation and breath to others.

# JARGON AND SHOPTALK

Jargon and shoptalk, used thoughtfully, can define a space and community as precisely as the setting, lighting, or any other design elements. In David Mamet's *Glengarry Glen Ross*, one understands very swiftly that the action is taking place among realtors. This information is communicated at least partially as a result of the jargon-heavy, coded language the characters employ. In his later play, *Speed-the-Plow*, a dense fog of movie speak envelopes the conversations and provides the context for the tense negotiations surrounding script and production.

Caution should be employed, however. Too much jargon or shoptalk can be alienating and create an impenetrable wall between your characters and the audience.

# LIMIT YOUR CHARACTERS

How many characters are too many? There was a time when a playwright could create a play with twenty or thirty different characters in the cast and get it produced. That time has passed.

Today, a cast of six represents a considerable expense for a theatre, and every character you add after that significantly diminishes the play's chances of ever receiving a production.

A good character is a wonderful thing, but if you wish to see your play produced you will exercise extreme caution as regards to the number you choose to employ in any given play.

# THE POWER OF THE
# VISUAL

Think, for just a moment, how much time and energy people spend watching. Watching their children. Watching other people at work. Watching themselves in reflected surfaces. Watching.

We are hyper aware of everything going on around us—we have to be. We would never have survived as a species all these millions of years if we weren't visually vigilant.

The result is, now, if you sit at a bus stop, you will find that you are aware of the smallest changes in others around you. If someone has a cold and their nose is running, you'll know. If someone stares at someone else a fraction of a second too long, you will be aware of the discomfort it causes, and if someone begins to cry, even if it's only quietly, their distress will be noted by everyone almost immediately.

We can't help it, and we can't halt it. We are built to observe, and we are continually drawing information from our surroundings. One of the reasons plays are so powerful is because they exploit this strength. They are meant to be *seen*, and it can be argued that the unspoken visual narrative is as important, and maybe more important, as the spoken narrative. In this sense, every single image of a play advances the story, and so every single image must be selected carefully.

If you attend the theatre in another country, a country where you don't speak the language, it's likely that you will still be able to determine much of what is happening on stage just by watching.

Spectacle—the striking, arresting visual image—has always played an important role in the theatre. The following are just a few notable examples where the visual image has played an unusually pivotal role.

# STUDY ONE—*RHINOCEROS* BY EUGÈNE IONESCO

The protagonist, Berenger, learns that a rhinoceros has stampeded through the street, crushing people underfoot. This is a singular enough event that at first it causes people to puzzle over where the animal might have come from. Gradually, however, Berenger makes the disconcerting discovery that people everywhere are actually, physically transforming into rhinos, and there appears to be no way of preventing it.

At first folks are horrified, but soon they come not only to accept the fact, but look forward to the change. Berenger watches with dismay as his closest friend transforms in front of him. In the end, the entire population is transfigured, all the citizens becoming uncaring, unthinking, brutal creatures.

The image of the rhinoceros—and of people *transformed*—is central to this play and says something about how the entire world can be altered and take a brutal turn in the blink of an eye.

# STUDY TWO—*K2* BY PATRICK MEYERS

A play entirely set on the side of a cliff of the second highest mountain in the world. The sheer visual bravura of positioning characters clinging to an icy ledge is energizing. As the play opens the audience is made to realize that two climbing partners have experienced a tragic accident. They must somehow survive as Taylor, one half of the duo, attempts to retrieve a climbing rope necessary to save himself and his injured climbing partner, Harold.

The brooding mountain comes to stand for the forces of antagonism that prevent these two from making their way to safety.

# STUDY THREE—
# *THE PERSECUTION AND ASSASSINATION OF JEAN-PAUL MARAT AS PERFORMED BY THE INMATES OF THE ASYLUM AT CHARENTON UNDER THE DIRECTION OF THE MARQUIS DE SADE*
# BY PETER WEISS

Through the device of a play within a play, *The Persecution and Assassination of Jean-Paul Marat* exploits a different, supremely theatrical form of spectacle. The play is situated within the terrible squalor of an asylum, and within that asylum a variety of disturbed patients gradually transform themselves as they take on the characters of the French Revolution.

The squalor, the scale, and the dramatic transformation of the inmates provide much of the vigour and visual energy of this contemporary classic.

# STUDY FOUR—*EINSTEIN'S GIFT* BY VERN THIESSEN

There is spectacle to be mined in the ironic juxtaposition of an iconic figure. Consider this duel between famed scientist and pacifist Albert Einstein and a contemporary of his, scientist Fritz Haber:

**HABER:** What would our beloved Bismarck say to this, eh Otto? If all Germans acted like Einstein, we'd have lost all Prussia.

*(to* ALBERT*)* Did you know that my uncle Ludwig viciously killed a samurai warrior?

**ALBERT:** Haber, I—

**HABER:** *(striking a fencing stance) En garde.*

*They fence.* HABER *is quite good. After a few passes they break.*

Well, well, not bad. Your Prussian school training didn't do you so bad. Let's see how you do battle on two fronts.

**ALBERT:** No, really, I—

**HABER:** *(going on the attack)* If the radiant energy emitted by a black body is infinitely divisible, what value can it have within a given range?

**ALBERT:** The energy emitted by a black body must always be an integral of a quantum and never less.

**HABER:** *(pressing)* What is the energy a single electron possesses when radiation with a frequency of one times ten to the fifteenth strikes sodium metal.

**177**

**ALBERT:** Four point one electron volts.

**HABER:** *(thrusting)* Light is a wave!

**ALBERT:** No! Its energy is only dependent on its frequency and therefore light is also a particle!

*ALBERT scores a hit.*

**HABER:** Ah!

*HABER drops his foil, clutching his cheek.**

# STUDY FIVE—*THE ISLAND* BY ATHOL FUGARD

At the beginning of this play about prisoners on Robben Island, South Africa's political prison during the days of apartheid, two Black men share a lengthy opening sequence during which they mime the digging of sand, the image described in the text as one of "back breaking and grotesquely futile labour." They mime digging, carting, and emptying the sand at the other's feet, and then commence digging again. Their labour is shown to be interminable. Following this, a whistle is blown. They are handcuffed and shackled together, forced to run, and after stumbling, they are beaten.

The silence, the simplicity, and the overwhelming sense of lives wasted imbues this sequence with tremendous power.

---

* Vern Thiessen, *Einstein's Gift* (Toronto: Playwrights Canada Press, 2003), 17–18.

# COMEDY

The subject of comedy is so immense that any serious analysis of it could take up a book all on its own. There are, however, a few things that may be touched on briefly.

Aristotle defined tragedy as drama that concerns folks of an elevated nature who struggle through stages from good fortune to bad, and who speak in a refined, poetic idiom. He proposed that comedy, on the other hand, concerned average folks who experienced a transition from bad circumstances to good, and spoke a more common vernacular.

Unfortunately, this definition, like so much of classical theory, is essentially useless to the person writing contemporary comedy—and not especially useful for the person writing tragedy either.

While a comedic play is intended to amuse an audience, it should not be mistaken for stand-up comedy material—though it may draw upon elements of the classic stand-up routine. Nor is a play sketch comedy either. In both stand-up and sketch comedy, the focus tends to be on the immediate laugh that arises out of a particular situation or observation. In a comedic play, the arc is longer. The comedy arises out of character applied to the specific context of story and struggle.

In fact, the structure of comedy as written for the theatre isn't so very different from that of drama written for the theatre because both forms are first and foremost embedded in a narrative. Just as the sober, reflective qualities of a drama arise out of the struggles of characters in a particularly serious kind of story, the lighter, comedic elements of a comedy arise out of the conflicts of characters in a particularly buoyant kind of story.

This is true even of the earliest comedies. In *The Frogs*, Aristophanes mines an unlikely, improbable situation—a god descends to the underworld to fetch a poet back to earth and in so doing hopes to restore poetry to its rightful place of prominence.

In this play, which spends so much time upsetting and debasing figures that were previously elevated, a good deal of the humour is bawdy. The god Dionysus himself is shown to be highly competitive as he plunges into an intense argument with a chorus of frogs in a swamp near Hades. This debate grows more pitched, with the god urging the frogs to silence and the frogs maintaining their right to sing. It is only when Dionysus releases a commanding fart that he finally silences them. The explosive blast, of course, is meant to contrast comically with the powers more commonly associated with gods, and it is important to recognize that it is employed as a strategy by Dionysus to achieve his desire in the context of this struggle.

# STUDY ONE—
# SOME ASSEMBLY REQUIRED
# BY EUGENE STICKLAND

The following scene from the play *Some Assembly Required* by Eugene Stickland provides a more contemporary example of comedy emerging from struggle.

In this Christmas comedy of family dysfunction, the desire of the eldest son at home for the holidays is simply to survive Christmas. That seemingly uncomplicated **desire** almost proves too demanding. Every action is so charged with **conflict** that even making the Christmas eggnog is fuel for mayhem. In the following scene, Walter attempts to make conversation with his brother Gordon, who has sequestered himself in a darkened basement with a vat of Christmas eggnog.

**GORDON:** *(handing WALTER a glass of eggnog)* Well, I made this eggnog myself, and I've been drinking it for days now, and my body hasn't tried to turn itself inside out so I think it's probably safe.

**WALTER:** No MSG?

**GORDON:** No. Do you need some?

**WALTER:** No. I shun MSG.

**GORDON:** Well, there's no MSG in this eggnog. This eggnog is the real thing.

**WALTER:** Kind of a strange texture there, Gord. How'd you make it?

**GORDON:** The normal way.

**WALTER:** What do you consider the normal way?

**GORDON:** Mix up rum and the eggs. Add a bit of nutmeg.

**WALTER:** Hmmm. Just the rum and the eggs, eh?

**GORDON:** Yeah.

**WALTER:** No milk?

**GORDON:** No. But nutmeg.

**WALTER:** How unusual.

**GORDON:** There's no law saying you have to have milk in eggnog, is there?

**WALTER:** No. Thousands of recipes suggest it, but probably no law says you actually have to have it . . . unfortunately.*

There are several very "funny lines" in this play, but that's not what the comedy of the play lives or dies upon. Rather, the focus of the play is

---

* Eugene Stickland, *Some Assembly Required* (Regina: Couteau Books, 1995), 18–19.

squarely upon the flaws of the characters and the strains in their relationships. As *Some Assembly Required* examines the relationships within a context of pressure, it expects comedy to emerge. Part of the comedy arises out of a **conflict** between forces of unusual and usual. Walter is perhaps a little odd himself, but in this case he acts as a kind of objective voice, attempting to understand and restore his highly unusual brother to a more common understanding of things.

So, Walter's gentle but persistent interrogation of his brother generates comedy, as does Gordon's stubborn refusal to acknowledge the necessity of any other ingredients but rum, nutmeg, and raw eggs in eggnog. Their inability to be direct with one another is as much a cause of the comedy as are the skewed ingredients of the faux eggnog.

# STUDY TWO—*KIM'S CONVENIENCE* BY INS CHOI

In this scene, Appa, the owner of Kim's Convenience Store, frustrated at the seeming inability of his daughter and her prospective boyfriend to expedite matters of the heart, elects to take direct action.

He employs his martial arts skills and applies a submission hold to compel Alex, the police officer boyfriend, to propose to his daughter, Janet. Then, when his daughter objects to this drastic and inappropriate intervention, Appa simultaneously applies a submission hold on her and attempts to force her to say yes. At this point, Alex surprises Appa, and reverses the submission hold, restraining Appa. While Appa is restrained, Alex uses the opportunity to open his heart to Janet, and the two young people agree to meet for a date the next day. Before he exits, Alex turns the hold on Appa over to Janet.

**ALEX:** Come here. Apply pressure right here.

*They transfer holding* APPA.

**APPA:** AH!

**ALEX:** Bye Janet.

**JANET:** Bye.

**ALEX:** Please don't hold this against me, Mr. Kim. I just needed to talk to your daughter.

**APPA:** Okay, see you.

*ALEX exits. Bell.*

Okay, Janet, enough is enough, let go.

**JANET:** Thank you.

**APPA:** You welcome. Now let go.

**JANET:** "Thank you . . . Janet."

*Beat.*

Repeat. After. Me.

**APPA:** What? Ah!

**JANET:** Repeat after me. "Thank you, Janet."

**APPA:** AH!

**JANET:** Repeat after me. "Thank you—"

**APPA:** You welcome.

**JANET:** Repeat after me! "Thank you, Janet!"

**APPA:** Ah! Ah! Okay, okay, okay. Thank you, Janet. Okay, enough is enough, let go.

**JANET:** "I'm sorry."

**APPA:** That's okay. Ah!

**JANET:** Repeat after me. "I'm sorry."

**APPA:** Ah! Okay, okay, I'm sorry.

**JANET:** "I love you, Janet. I love you, Janet."

*Beat.*

"I love you, Janet!"

**APPA:** Ah! Okay! I love you, Janet!

*JANET releases APPA.*

**JANET:** I love you too, Appa. *(with arms open)* And see, no one's twisting my arms to say it.

*JANET slowly lowers her arms, picks up her bags, and walks to the back of the store.*

**APPA:** You were fourteen years old.

*JANET stops.*

You were fourteen years old, school project. "What I am most proud of." You write story how we begin store. Then you take picture of me in front of store. That is my most happy memory, Janet. I don't want you take over store. I want you live life best way you choosing.

*JANET takes the garbage bag from the closet and approaches the front door.*

Yah.

APPA *takes it from her.*

Go upstair. Go. Sleep.

JANET *embraces* APPA.

Okay, okay, okay, that's good enough, let go, Janet.*

In this scene the comedy arises, as so much comedy does, out of reversals. Appa, the father who appears to substantially misunderstand his daughter and habitually offers her unwelcome advice, is compelled to instead express his feelings, and in turn hear that his daughter loves him. These forced displays of affection result in the subsequent, more genuine emotional offerings moments later, which, in turn, results in recognition and reconciliation.

It's again worth noting the resilience that is ever present in comedy. Although Hapkido holds are applied liberally throughout the scene, there is no lasting scarring or suffering as a result. The characters bounce back, better than ever.

# STUDY THREE—
# THE IMPORTANCE OF BEING
# EARNEST BY OSCAR WILDE

In this notorious scene, one of the most famous confrontations in comedic theatre, we see Jack attempting to obtain permission from Gwendolen's mother for her daughter's hand in marriage.

**LADY BRACKNELL:** *(sitting down)* You can take a seat, Mr. Worthing.

*Looks in her pocket for note-book and pencil.*

---

* Ins Choi, *Kim's Convenience* (Toronto: House of Anansi Press, 2012), 78–80.

**185**

**JACK:** Thank you, Lady Bracknell, I prefer standing.

**LADY BRACKNELL:** *(pencil and note-book in hand)* I feel bound to tell you that you are not down on my list of eligible young men, although I have the same list as the dear Duchess of Bolton has. We work together, in fact. However, I am quite ready to enter your name, should your answers be what a really affectionate mother requires. Do you smoke?

**JACK:** Well, yes, I must admit I smoke.

**LADY BRACKNELL:** I am glad to hear it. A man should always have an occupation of some kind. There are far too many idle men in London as it is. How old are you?

**JACK:** Twenty-nine.

**LADY BRACKNELL:** A very good age to be married at. I have always been of the opinion that a man who desires to get married should know either everything or nothing. Which do you know?

**JACK:** *(after some hesitation)* I know nothing, Lady Bracknell.

**LADY BRACKNELL:** I am pleased to hear it. I do not approve of any-thing that tampers with natural ignorance. Ignorance is like a delicate exotic fruit; touch it and the bloom is gone. The whole theory of modern education is radically unsound. Fortunately in England, at any rate, education produces no effect whatsoever. If it did, it would prove a serious danger to the upper classes, and probably lead to acts of violence in Grosvenor Square. What is your income?

**JACK:** Between seven and eight thousand a year.

**LADY BRACKNELL:** *(makes a note in her book)* In land, or in investments?

**JACK:** In investments, chiefly.

**LADY BRACKNELL:** That is satisfactory. What between the duties expected of one during one's lifetime, and the duties exacted from one after one's death, land has ceased to be either a profit or a pleasure. It gives one position, and prevents one from keeping it up.

That's all that can be said about land.

**JACK:** I have a country house with some land, of course, attached to it, about fifteen hundred acres, I believe; but I don't depend on that for my real income. In fact, as far as I can make out, the poachers are the only people who make anything out of it.

**LADY BRACKNELL:** A country house! How many bedrooms? Well, that point can be cleared up afterwards. You have a town house, I hope?

A girl with a simple, unspoiled nature, like Gwendolen, could hardly be expected to reside in the country.

**JACK:** Well, I own a house in Belgrave Square, but it is let by the year to Lady Bloxham. Of course, I can get it back whenever I like, at six months' notice.

**LADY BRACKNELL:** Lady Bloxham? I don't know her.

**JACK:** Oh, she goes about very little. She is a lady considerably advanced in years.

**LADY BRACKNELL:** Ah, nowadays that is no guarantee of respectability of character. What number in Belgrave Square?

**JACK:** 149.

**LADY BRACKNELL:** *(shaking her head)* The unfashionable side. I thought there was something. However, that could easily be altered.

**JACK:** Do you mean the fashion, or the side?

**LADY BRACKNELL:** *(sternly)* Both, if necessary, I presume. What are your politics?

**JACK:** Well, I am afraid I really have none. I am a Liberal Unionist.

**LADY BRACKNELL:** Oh, they count as Tories. They dine with us. Or come in the evening, at any rate. Now to minor matters. Are your parents living?

**JACK:** I have lost both my parents.

**LADY BRACKNELL:** To lose one parent, Mr. Worthing, may be regarded as a misfortune; to lose both looks like carelessness. Who was your father? He was evidently a man of some wealth. Was he born in what the Radical papers call the purple of commerce, or did he rise from the ranks of the aristocracy?

**JACK:** I am afraid I really don't know. The fact is, Lady Bracknell, I said I had lost my parents. It would be nearer the truth to say that my parents seem to have lost me . . . I don't actually know who I am by birth. I was . . . well, I was found.

**LADY BRACKNELL:** Found!

**JACK:** The late Mr. Thomas Cardew, an old gentleman of a very charitable and kindly disposition, found me, and gave me the name of Worthing, because he happened to have a first-class ticket for Worthing in his pocket at the time. Worthing is a place in Sussex. It is a seaside resort.

**LADY BRACKNELL:** Where did the charitable gentleman who had a first-class ticket for this seaside resort find you?

**JACK:** *(gravely)* In a hand-bag.

**LADY BRACKNELL:** A hand-bag?

**JACK:** *(very seriously)* Yes, Lady Bracknell. I was in a hand-bag—a somewhat large, black leather hand-bag, with handles to it—an ordinary hand-bag in fact.

**LADY BRACKNELL:** In what locality did this Mr. James, or Thomas, Cardew come across this ordinary hand-bag?

**JACK:** In the cloak-room at Victoria Station. It was given to him in mistake for his own.

**LADY BRACKNELL:** The cloak-room at Victoria Station?

**JACK:** Yes. The Brighton line.

**LADY BRACKNELL:** The line is immaterial. Mr. Worthing, I confess I feel somewhat bewildered by what you have just told me. To be born, or at any rate bred, in a hand-bag, whether it had handles or not, seems to me to display a contempt for the ordinary decencies of family life that reminds one of the worst excesses of the French Revolution. And I presume you know what that unfortunate movement led to? As for the particular locality in which the hand-bag was found, a cloak-room at a railway station might serve to conceal a social indiscretion—has probably, indeed, been used for that purpose before now—but it could hardly be regarded as an assured basis for a recognized position in good society.

**JACK:** May I ask you then what you would advise me to do? I need hardly say I would do anything in the world to ensure Gwendolen's happiness.

**LADY BRACKNELL:** I would strongly advise you, Mr. Worthing, to try and acquire some relations as soon as possible, and to make a definite effort to produce at any rate one parent, of either sex, before the season is quite over.

**JACK:** Well, I don't see how I could possibly manage to do that. I can produce the hand-bag at any moment. It is in my dressing-room at home. I really think that should satisfy you, Lady Bracknell.

**LADY BRACKNELL:** Me, sir! What has it to do with me? You can hardly imagine that I and Lord Bracknell would dream of allowing our only daughter—a girl brought up with the utmost care—to marry into a cloak-room, and form an alliance with a parcel? Good morning, Mr. Worthing!

*LADY BRACKNELL sweeps out in majestic indignation.**

It's easy to recognize many of the elements that have been previously discussed: a **character** acting upon a **desire**, another **character** testing and opposing that **character**, increasing complication, increasing intensity, and a dramatic reversal. These elements propel the narrative of *The Importance of Being Earnest.*

But what elements make it distinctly comedic? Here are a few constituent parts that bear consideration.

1. *Tone*

The entire tone of *The Importance of Being Earnest* is light. It is impossible to read a passage such as Lady Bracknell's " . . . Ignorance is like a delicate exotic fruit; touch it and the bloom is gone. The whole theory of modern education is radically unsound. Fortunately in England, at any rate, education produces no effect whatsoever . . . " without receiving the message that a joke is being shared.

2. *The Improbable Treated as Entirely Probable*

In the same way that Dionysus doesn't find anything improbable about fetching Euripides from Hades to elevate the level of culture on earth, Lady Bracknell may find the notion that Jack was left in a handbag in a train disagreeable—but she doesn't question the probability.

---

* Oscar Wilde, *The Importance of Being Earnest* (London: Nick Hern Books, 1995), 18–22.

### 3. An Ability to Withstand Punishment Without Suffering

Like the characters in cartoons that are hit by hammers or blown up by dynamite and seem to suffer little harm, characters in comedy are remarkably resilient. They may complain, and they may suffer—but the agony is not sustained.

### 4. An Intense, Unyielding Desire

Though the odds may be against the character, the pursuit of their desire is unyielding, almost to the point of approaching an obsession. This is as true of Molière's Miser in the play of the same name, as it is of Senior Armado in *Love's Labour's Lost*. The French theorist Henri Bergson, in his discussion of humour in his essay "Laughter," characterized this failure to compensate for realities and obstacles as a kind of "mechanical inelasticity" and suggested that it was an important component in comedy.

### 5. Complication is Frequently of a High Order

Although this is not true of all comedies, nor is it *only* true of comedies (mysteries for instance frequently manifest a high degree of complexity as well), it is true that comedies often display highly complicated plots. This is true of very early plays—*The Menaechmi*, for instance, which became *A Comedy of Errors*, which also became the basis for *A Funny Thing Happened On The Way to the Forum*—as well as more contemporary works such as *Travesties* by Tom Stoppard and *The Producers* by Mel Brooks. All share as a central feature a very high degree of complication.

### 6. Speed

Although pace and tempo are important factors in every play, comedies, like cheetahs, tend to be built for speed. Perhaps because humour arises out of the unexpected turn of event, a languid comedy is a rare occurrence.

# ADAPTATIONS

*A great novel does not necessarily make a great play. The two are very different beasts.*
—Sarah Hemming, "Adapting Novels for the Theatre"*

There is a long, long history of adapting literary works for the theatre. When William Shakespeare wrote *A Comedy of Errors*, he was adapting *The Menaechmi*, previously written by the ancient Roman playwright, Plautus, and Plautus in his turn was busy adapting the much earlier work of a variety of ancient Greek comic playwrights, most notably the prolific comic writer Menander. And who knows what Menander was adapting.

The novels of Charles Dickens have long been transformed into common fare for the stage—*Oliver Twist*, *The Mystery of Edwin Drood*, *Nicholas Nickleby*, and, of course, most famously and ever-so-regularly, *A Christmas Carol*.

Recent years have witnessed an increased interest in adaptations, however. *Wolf Hall*, *The Curious Incident of the Dog in The Night-Time*, *War Horse*, *Les Misérables*, *Middlemarch*, and *Wicked* are just a few novels that have found their way onto the stage. This may reflect the interdisciplinary interests of a new generation. It may also reflect the insecurity felt by those who administer theatre companies in these economically uncertain times and their wish to capitalize on the name recognition of literary works that have already proven themselves successful. Whatever the

---

* Sarah Hemming, "Adapting Novels for the Theatre," *Financial Times*, 22 November 2013, https://www.ft.com/content/30392f4c-5130-11e3-b499-00144feabdc0.

reason, the interest in adaptations is genuine and has had a genuine impact on the theatre.

I spoke with playwright Vern Thiessen, who recently enjoyed great success with his adaptation of Somerset Maugham's *Of Human Bondage*. I asked him how the process of adaptation differs from writing an originally sourced play.

"The most important questions you must answer," he says, "when adapting from another source are: Why Me? Why This? and Why Now? Answering these questions will lead you to discover:

1. Why your adaptation is unique to your own voice and vision.

2. Why this work needs to be heard in this form (i.e., drama).

3. Why it is relevant/important for the audience to attend and witness.

"Answering these questions, for me, drives the adaptation into the present moment that is the touchstone of live theatre. Answering these questions forces you to make choices on what parts of the original material you are going to adapt, why you are doing it, and how you are going to do it. Staying true to the spirit of the original while staying true to your own voice is the tightrope you must walk.

"And don't bother trying to copy and paste," he advises. "You can't slap the book down on the page and think it will sing on the stage."

Aaron Bushkowsky, another playwright who has experienced success adapting works for the stage, (*Farewell, My Lovely*; *The Big Sleep*) observed that, "The worst thing to do when adapting a novel to the stage is to follow a chapter by chapter plot because you will soon be overrun with characters, minute plot points, and needless exposition. Novels contain so much backstory and explanation while theatre needs to remain in the present.

"The best thing you can do is read the novel a number of times, write down a loose plot, and identify major characters . . . then throw the book in the drawer and start writing your play."

# STUDY ONE—*OF HUMAN BONDAGE*, ADAPTED FROM W. SOMERSET MAUGHAM'S NOVEL OF THE SAME NAME BY VERN THIESSEN

*CAREY alone.*

*The company enter, each their own work of art.*

**TYRELL:** "Oh, God, Thou has appointed me to watch over the life and death of Thy creatures.

**TYRELL/CAREY:** Here am I, ready for my vocation, and now I turn unto my calling."

**TYRELL:** This is your oath.

*One by one, the company slowly come alive, populating and creating the landscape of this place.*

Your work here at St. Luke's will be tedious and interesting. It will be trivial and complex. You will see joy and despair, tears and laughter, happiness and woe. You will see wretched women and helpless children. You will witness men seized by drink and its inevitable price. Death sighs in these rooms. And birth cries just as well.

*TYRELL moves among them.*

You are the artist and your patients are like clay. Like a painter, you will note the texture of their skin and the colour of their eyes. You will discover who they are by the way they speak. You will know their trade by the way they walk. You will see the mask of their humanity rudely torn off, exposing the raw soul.

*Only* CAREY *remains lost and still.*

Here there is neither good nor bad, neither right nor wrong. Here there is only life. And as you will one day swear: "In purity and holiness, guard this life and this art." Next!*

In this stylized beginning, Thiessen ignores the earlier chapters of the novel with its painful exploration of Carey's childhood, his mother's death, his barren, bored life with his joyless aunt and uncle, the torments he experiences at the hands of bullies as a young boy, and, instead, propels the audience into Carey's adult world, where the stakes become high and where his romantic attachments—the bondage of the title—begin. It's interesting, however, to consider how this introduction stays true to the *sensibility* of the novel, while at the same time totally abandoning the *form* of the novel.

---

* Vern Thiessen, *Of Human Bondage* (Toronto: Playwrights Canada Press, 2016), 3–4.

# IMPROVISATION

Improvisation has been an integral part of theatre for as long as theatre has been practised. The sixteenth and seventeenth century comic troupes of the *commedia dell'arte* employed stock characters, athletic turns, and broadly comic situations in their improvisational work, and in so doing knit together a series of comedic scenarios that had the capacity to incorporate and adapt the recent events, gossip, and political speculation of the communities and cities they performed in.

Many contemporary writers employ improvisational devices as a catalyst to generate dialogue and character. Writing can, in and of itself, be viewed as a kind of improvisational exercise. We make offers on the page, and then accept and develop them. But for some creators, the improvisational exercise extends beyond the initial stages of exploration or shaping. Recently, Mischief Theatre, a British group devoted to improvisation, leaned upon their improvisational comedic training and skill set to develop a wild romp in which an amateur theatre company stages, badly, a whodunit. That play, titled, accurately, *The Play That Goes Wrong*, went on to capture Best New Comedy at the Laurence Olivier Awards in London and then later a Tony Award in New York.

Writer, director, and performer Rebecca Northan has employed the improvisational process in a slightly different way. She has generated a number of very successful works, each one rising out of a similar improvisational impulse. She calls the kind of work she does "spontaneous theatre."

Her initial venture into this form was the play *Blind Date*, performed first in 2007 for the Harbourfront Centre's Spiegel Show in Toronto. In *Blind Date*, a clown character named Mimi appears on stage and selects someone from the audience to join her for their mutual "blind date." The narrative of the piece conforms to a kind of loose dramatic arc—there is the struggle between the two on stage to establish a kind of intimacy, to make their encounter meaningful, to somehow make the blind date successful. The metatheatrical nature of the exercise endows the performance with a unique dramatic tension and nervous energy—the audience is completely unable to predict how things will unfold because they know that half of the blind date is one of "them," untrained, unrehearsed, a regular Joe pulled from the audience without any performance skills. Perhaps, the audience thinks, the performance will all go drastically awry.

A hallmark of spontaneous theatre is taking care of the guest. Rebecca's skill as a performer and improvisor permits the invited visitor to relax, to abandon their fear of embarrassment, to engage in the date, forget that others are watching, and allow a delicate, often surprising, always funny tale to emerge.

Since *Blind Date* was first performed, Rebecca has presented her spontaneous theatre creation hundreds of times in assorted cities and has hired other clowns to take on the role of Mimi and improvise this romantic encounter in multiple locations.

Rebecca has since that time employed the spontaneous form to create other hybrid performances that are one part pre-arranged scenario, and one part unplanned, improvisational impulse. These shows, like *Blind Date*, employ a rough structure based around a narrative core—a fantastical adventure (*Legend Has It*), a detective mystery (*Undercover*), Shakespearean style theatre, (*An Undiscovered Shakespeare*)—then recruit a member of the audience to actively participate, making critical decisions throughout, and consequently altering and amending the direction of the story in each performance.

# PART EIGHT
## KEYBOARD EXERCISES

# EXERCISES

Famed playwright Christopher Durang has said, "Students seem to love the idea of [writing] exercises. Exercises are almost like taking a doctor's prescription and filling it at the pharmacy. They suggest that through games and tricks you can find out how to write a good play. I find myself distrustful of them . . . "*

He is, of course, absolutely correct. Writing exercises can't magically enable anyone to write a good play. Nothing can do that.

What exercises can do is allow a person to become aware of new strategies to employ in their writing.

Students of writing who are anxious about working with autobiographical material may change their minds after successfully crafting a scene based on remembered past events. A student who was previously unaware of the power of subtext may learn to utilize a more subtle approach.

Writing isn't a science, and there is no formula that if followed will produce literary enlightenment. But by working through exercises, an individual can develop a different set of creative muscles.

Some of the exercises described in the following pages are meant for a writer to try on their own. Some are meant to be practiced in a group setting (although with some small adjustments they can be practised independently as well). Almost all of the exercises are enriched if they are shared and discussed in some form of a writing group.

---

* Christopher Durang, "Seven Sure-fire Exercises to Lead Your Inner Playwright to Inspiration," *atPlay Newsletter*, Spring/Summer 2005.

# EXERCISE ONE—
# STORY IN A BOX

**Step One**

This is an interesting foundational exercise because it has so many different applications, because it's easy to execute, and because it can be so enjoyable.

It's best performed within a small group (if you are working on your own, simply read this portion over and then move on to perform Step Two) and the premise is simple. Each person in the group is asked to select an actual event from their past that they are willing to share aloud with the rest of the group. The event selected should be based on something that has been either witnessed or experienced firsthand, and should have had some kind of strong emotional impact on the storyteller. It could have been a joyful experience, or a frightening one, or awe-inspiring, embarrassing—doesn't matter. The story should take no longer than five minutes to tell.

Before sharing the story, the participants should take time to recollect how the event actually occurred. Determine where the event began, what exactly happened, and how it ended. Then the participants should select or create three objects—photos, drawings, clay models—that will visually represent some element of the beginning, middle, and end of the story. These objects should be placed in a box or a bag.

Gather in a group, and one after another have each participant relate their story. Each person should reveal the objects they have placed in their box at the point in the story that they deem most effective.

POINTS OF ATTENTION

Take the time after the stories have been shared to debrief and examine the following elements:

1. Pay close attention to the notion of struggle. Often there are several levels of **conflict** embedded in these stories. **Struggle** is integral to the nature of the narrative, of course ("I remember once I was lost and had to find my way out of the woods . . . "). **Struggle** can often be found in the actual telling of the story, however, and it is important to understand how volatile narrative is, how difficult it can be for the presenter to engage with emotional material. This is an incredibly useful lesson for a playwright. How often have I read scenes written by novice playwrights where emotional content of the most wrenching variety was handled in a cavalier fashion. How often I have wished that the writers had undergone an exercise of this sort so that they might have considered the kind of minefield people work their way through when attempting to express themselves truthfully.

2. Watch carefully for where you feel the audience is paying attention. It's useful to understand where an audience connects and disconnects.

3. Watch and listen to how the words of the story are connected to the content and purpose of the story. There are lessons to be learned about **style** and **tone** and how they evolve out of **purpose** and **content**.

4. Pay attention to how emotion develops in the story. There may very well be matters of intellect to deal with in the narrative, but every story is a kind of emotional journey, and it's worth noting that emotions tend to intensify both for the characters and the audience in **parallel** as the **crisis** and **climax** approaches.

5. There are interesting things to be learned about how characters truly speak. It is fascinating to observe the distinct kinds of language used by each individual storyteller. Each story is delivered in a specific manner, and the use of language changes over the course of the story. This can, if one allows it, become a bit of a clinic into authentic dialogue.

6. The exercise is one that allows the participants to become aware of the intimate connection between the story and the audience and allows each individual to experience that sensation and tension from the vantage points of active participant and spectator.

7. The exercise employs a **minimalist** approach to spectacle—only a few simple visual aids are utilized—but pay attention to how even these rudimentary images augment and elevate the story. Sometimes even small gestures can have a lasting impact.

8. The exercise allows you to examine the connection between the process of reportage—which we do every day as we relate events to others—and the process of playwriting.

**Step Two**

After performing the previous exercise, the participants should select another incident from their past, only this time they should use it as the basis for a written scene.

Again, participants must carefully select the **incident**, and consider how it began, developed, and unfolded—but in this case, participants should understand that they, not the events themselves, are in charge of the **structure**. They are responsible for shaping the scene as they write it. The event is simply the catalyst or inspiration.

They have total liberty to fill in blanks that exist, create characters where necessary, and alter any portion as they see fit.

This is a useful exercise for developing an understanding of the synthesis between memory and craft in playwriting.

Follow this up with a short reading from any one of a number of autobiographical works, and if possible access the notes or journals of the writer to see how past events shaped the scene, and in what respect the play differed from the historical actualities.

It's interesting, for instance, to read the play *Rhinoceros* by Eugène Ionesco, and then consult his journals detailing his thoughts about Europe as it descended into fascism and brutality.

POINTS OF ATTENTION

1. Consider, or discuss if you are part of a writing group, how difficult, or easy, it is to create a scene from memory. It may be both, simultaneously, in different ways.

2. Consider or discuss the kind of responsibility participants have toward recollected events. Is it ever possible to be absolutely faithful to the events of a story? Isn't there always some negotiation and editing that occurs?

3. Reflect on the sensation that comes with changing events. Sometimes it can feel very freeing to return to a memory and rewrite it. The understanding that one is not bound to past events, but that history is just a source, can be very liberating.

# EXERCISE TWO—
# THE PLAYWRIGHT
# AS OBSERVER

*"I heard two Russians in a muddled conversation about pessimism, a conversation that solved nothing; all I am bound to do is reproduce that conversation exactly as I heard it."*\*
—Anton Chekhov

This particular exercise is also best taught, or experienced, in two parts.

**Step One**

The creation of sharp dialogue—and by that I mean dialogue that is effective, active, succinct, and distinct—can only be truly learned through listening. Great dialogue captures the nuances, rhythms, and idioms of a variety of individuals. If you hope to achieve this, you must first know how people—people other than *you*—speak. How does one develop this skill? One way is to venture out and eavesdrop.

Start now. Pick up a pen and paper. Travel to any place where you are likely to overhear entire conversations without much difficulty. Cafés with tables pushed close together are good. Buses and subways are terrific. Bars

---

\* Chekhov, "Anton Chekhov on Writing."

can be excellent, provided they're not too noisy. Sporting events, church sermons, hospital waiting rooms, or political rallies—they can all work.

Sit down, listen, and write. Try not to be intrusive. Attempt to capture *whole* conversations—a snippet won't provide you with as much information. It is important that you record what is being done as well as what is being said, and it is wise to make note of the environment and context as well.

Before you race out with pen and pad, however, let me provide you with some sage advice regarding this assignment.

I knew of one group of students that travelled to a bar frequented by a rather tough crowd. These students parked themselves at a table and began their work. They weren't entirely certain that they were catching every word, so *they drew their table closer.* They sketched a few drawings of some of their subjects so they would recollect the events more completely.

Now, this element of society tends to be very sensitive about this kind of scrutiny. First it makes them anxious, then it makes them testy.

In a very short time the students' activities were brought to the attention of a couple of very burly leather-clad individuals who confronted the students, knocked over the table, and chased them out into the street.

I would caution you to *be discreet.* This is not only a quality to cultivate for this particular exercise, but an attribute that will help you your whole life through.

POINTS OF ATTENTION

1. The intent of the exercise is to make one aware of qualities of voice. How are things phrased by different individuals? How does each person use words differently? Is it possible to determine who is talking simply by the use of their words, and the phrasing?

2. What kind of language does the group you observed share? Are there terms that they use in a specific and distinct way? What are you able to tell about them from their vocabulary? Are you able to establish anything about their background from their choice of words? Their employment? Their nationality? Their neighbourhood?

3. On a very basic level, how grammatical is the conversation? Do people speak in whole sentences, or do they use incomplete phrases? Do they finish every sentence or leave some sentences incomplete? How is the conversation shared? Is it equitable? How does a person gain permission to speak?

4. Become aware of qualities of hierarchy and class. In North America we tend to believe that there is no such thing as class, but a subtle pecking order exists in almost every human endeavour. Some playwrights are more observant of these qualities than others. Harold Pinter, for instance, is especially aware that in the smallest communications there is an almost invisible hierarchy at work.

5. Ask yourself, "Why are these individuals talking?" "What do these people want from each other?" Bear in mind that no one ever does anything for nothing—so what are these individuals trying to achieve through the use of all these words? Are their intentions conveyed explicitly, or through subtext, or both?

6. Become aware of rhythm and cadence. Some individuals speak in long flowing sentences, others use a choppy, direct structure. Sometimes conversations will themselves shift in rhythm, moving from an easy exchange to a more excited, intense discussion.

**Step Two**

Now, with your rough material in hand to use as the source, write a scene based upon your observations. Try as much as possible to utilize the raw materials—the dialogue, actions, observations regarding location and environment. Some elements may draw your attention more than others. Perhaps a relationship you witnessed will form the basis of your scene. Perhaps it is the kind of language used that will have had the greatest impact upon you. Whatever elements you embrace, remember that *you* are the writer. It is your responsibility to take this material and shape it. The scene you construct must function dramatically and make sense as a scene. It's not sufficient to simply lay the material out and say, "That's the way I heard it, so that's the way it goes." An audience won't accept that, and you shouldn't either.

This material is like pliant clay in a potter's hands. It's the job of the writer to carefully shape the rough material into a vessel that will contain the narrative content.

POINTS OF ATTENTION

1. This exercise tends to lead students to craft dialogue that feels distinct and authentic, and it is worth examining again what qualities make the dialogue seem this way.

2. The exercise reminds us of what is said and done—and what isn't. Often people who participate in this exercise are surprised by how much is unsaid by the people they observed.

3. Perhaps most importantly, the exercise causes students to perceive the world in a new way. Instead of desperately trying to invent **story**, invent **situation**, invent **character**, a person begins to understand that there are stories, characters, and situations happening every day, all around them.

# EXERCISE THREE—WRITING
# UNDER THE SCENE

In real life almost nothing is easy or simple.

Take talking, for instance. Novice writers often create dialogue as though it was the easiest thing in the world for people to speak their mind. But it's not. If it was easy to merely tell someone something, it would be the first thing that people do, but instead it's often the last. People stew endlessly about how best to inform friends, family, or neighbours about issues that they regard as delicate, sensitive, or troubling.

Consider how difficult it is to tell someone that you love them—if you're not sure that they will return those feelings. Think about how challenging it is to confront someone and tell them you hate them—if they're a little bit scary and crazy. Recall the last time it was necessary to confess an error or indiscretion, and the effort that was attached to that endeavour. Recollect how potentially treacherous it can be to give anyone any kind of advice, even simple advice. Sure, we all know how to talk, but that doesn't make the activity easy.

This exercise explores that premise. It asks that you write a scene for two characters. Ensure that a strong **desire** is present within the scene, and a **conflict**.

Now, write the scene without ever once allowing your characters to actually and explicitly discuss their objectives. Make absolutely certain that these characters continue advancing their agendas, ensure that they apply new strategies as the previous ones fail. But do not, absolutely do not, allow them to talk about their desires.

Like all interesting exercises, this permits one to see the world from a different perspective. Do it a few times, and it will become possible to observe how in real life people are taunting, testing, intimidating, praising, persuading, seducing, cautioning, comforting others all the time without ever actually explicitly articulating their feelings or desires.

There are a number of writers who are especially talented in this regard. It's worth reading the work of Sam Shepard, for instance, to see how effectively he employs this technique in his writing.

POINTS OF ATTENTION

1. Have a look at places where it is especially effective not to articulate a desire. Are there instances when *not* saying something is more effective than saying it?

2. Often, after observing a scene written in this fashion, participants will be able to recollect seeing other similar examples of people pursuing goals in an indirect fashion. Discuss these examples.

3. Although what isn't being said is important, sometimes what is being said or done is especially effective as a complementary metaphor. As a (mediocre) example of this, a person who is trying to explain something difficult may be peeling and coring an apple. The act of getting past the surface and moving to the centre of something may be useful to you. Pay close attention to the activities and utterances of your characters.

# EXERCISE FOUR—
# LIMIT THE WORDS

This exercise follows the previous one quite naturally. The participant is asked to craft a scene ensuring that something of importance is at stake, and that the characters within the scene are working hard to achieve their desires. But this time, don't allow any of the characters to utilize sentences with more than three words.

POINTS OF ATTENTION

1. Have a look at what happens to the rhythm of the text when you use this exercise. Is there a cadence that becomes evident?

2. Pay attention to how this alters the pace of the story. How vigorously do the characters apply themselves to their objectives?

3. What does this exercise do to the characters? Do they present in a distinct fashion as a result of the way they use words?

Content is important, but how words are placed, arranged, and constructed within sentences has tremendous impact as well.

A variation on this exercise is to permit one character to speak in sentences of no more than three words, and the other in sentences of no less than ten. Examine how this alters the rhythm and pace of the scene. Be attentive to how distinct the characters become on the basis of their contrasting speech patterns.

# EXERCISE FIVE—
# NO WORDS

The previous exercises have dealt, in one way or another, with the power of words when limited or manipulated a certain way. This exercise examines the potential that exists in communicating through the visual.

Write a scene with a definite beginning, middle, and end, and with clear goals and objectives—only this time don't allow the characters to speak at all.

Part of the challenge is to prevent the scene from descending into pantomime or charades. Consider just how much of what is performed among humans is done without words. Think through the circumstances that might allow a character to attempt to achieve something without speaking.

Try to be as truthful to the given circumstances as possible.

POINTS OF ATTENTION

1. How much power, tension, anxiety, and mystery can be generated by the denial of speech?

2. What devices serve to hold an audience's attention when dialogue is absent?

3. Is it possible to tell a clear story without the characters using dialogue? What strengths lie in this approach?

An interesting variation on this exercise is to allow no more than three lines of dialogue in the entire scene. What happens when dialogue is withheld and used only sparingly? What kind of importance are the words given? What kind of tension can be created?

# EXERCISE SIX—
# ROUTINE AND RITUAL

Routine activities take up a good deal of our lives: vacuuming, dish-washing, cooking, dressing, undressing, showering, applying makeup, brushing teeth, buying groceries, paying bills, doing taxes, setting the table, clearing the table. It could be argued that routine activities take up the lion's share of our lives.

Likewise, consider all the time spent in rituals: dressing up for Halloween, presenting gifts on birthdays, attending funerals, anniver-saries, marriages, recognition dinners, graduations, proms, baptisms, bar mitzvahs, confirmations.

The wonderful thing about integrating a routine or a ritual into a scene is that the script, in a sense, writes itself. All the steps and stages of the ritual or routine must be observed and in a specific sequence. There's power in recognizing and acknowledging that process. When one incorpo-rates a routine or ritual activity into a scene, the audience may experience immediate and powerful feelings of empathy that accompany a sensation of familiarity.

But, there's another kind of power that is at the disposal of the writer, and that is the power that emerges when one breaks or bends the routine or ritual.

I once was seated in a restaurant when a birthday cake was brought in, candles burning, waiters singing. The cake was paraded through the restaurant to a table in the far corner where a large extended family was gathered, waiting. Everyone in the restaurant applauded and offered their congratulations. Shortly after everyone had returned to their dinners, we became aware of voices rising in anger. I turned and saw a young lady suddenly stand away from her table. As she stood, she shouted, "Well! It's not a very happy birthday for me!" Then she plunged a knife into the centre of the birthday cake. Following this she burst into tears and fled the restaurant. A young man stood, looked around at all the people staring at him—the entire restaurant, of course—then rushed out to find the young lady.

That moment was completely charged. I doubt that anyone who was there will ever forget that image of the knife being thrust into the centre of the cake.

There is energy attendant when one alters or interrupts a routine.

Try it. Construct a scene around a routine activity or a ritual and break or alter the routine or ritual in some way.

POINTS OF ATTENTION

1. How does using a routine or ritual also inform the content of the scene? Or does it? Is it possible to construct a scene in which the content is at odds with the routine or ritual?

2. How does the introduction of an "interruption" shape the structure of the scene? Or does it? Does it matter where the interruption occurs?

3. Consider how many plays have utilized rituals. *Cyrano de Bergerac* begins with the opening of a play, and then interrupts it when Cyrano demands that the show be closed. *Richard III* features a funeral procession, and then interrupts it when Richard woos the grieving widow.

# EXERCISE SEVEN—
# THE MONOLOGUE

There is a lot to be learned from spending time with a single character.
As a writer, it's easy to escape hard or uncomfortable writing situations by staying light on your feet. You shift from one character to another, one voice to another, one scene to another—and you are never really forced to dig deep into the core of your characters.

And yet, there is strength to be found by sticking with one individual and exploring that person fully. Working on a monologue will allow you to develop a character's authentic voice and it will force you to become more closely acquainted with the past, present, and future of that character. Listen to Braidie from Joan MacLeod's *The Shape of a Girl*.

**BRAIDIE:** I woke up this morning to this sound. This sound that feels far away one second then from right inside my gut the next. Very pure with the potential to be extremely creepy. But before I've even opened my eyes this other thing worms its way in and wreaks its usual havoc: the voice of Mum.

*The Shape of a Girl* is a play written as an extended monologue. Playwright Joan MacLeod maintains that she explores every play she writes as a series of monologues first until she gets the voices "right"— and only then does she proceed. Here's Braidie again.

217

**BRAIDIE:** The human body is what? Eighty percent water? That kills me. We're like these melons with arms and legs. Well eighty percent of the female brain is pure crap. We're constantly checking each other out, deciding who goes where, who's at the bottom.

When I look at her picture, when I look at the picture of the dead girl in the paper, part of me gets it. And I hate it that I do; I hate to be even partly composed of that sort of information. But right now, if you put me in a room filled with girls, girls my age that I've never seen before in my life—I could divide them all up. I could decide who goes where and just where I fit in without anyone even opening their mouth. They could be from this island, they could be from Taiwan. It doesn't matter. Nobody would have to say a word.*

Of course, not all plays will be, or should be, constructed around one voice. Nevertheless, staying with one character for an extended period of time allows the audience to engage with them in a special way.

The monologue can act as a direct portal to an interior, hidden portion of a character. Consider 10 (Bobbie James) in Jordan Tannahill's *Concord Floral*. Tricked by schoolmates into stripping at a party, then robbed of her clothing and forced to walk home naked, these are her shattered interior thoughts.

**10:** *(crying)* I remember thinking
The moment before I opened my eyes:
"You're not here"
"This is not really happening to you"
"Erase yourself"
"No one can see you"
"Erase yourself erase yourself"
"erase, erase, erase, erase—"
"If no one can see you, then you're not really naked"
"You're not really alone, they're not really cruel"
And when I opened my eyes I was gone
I wasn't there

---

* Joan MacLeod, *The Shape of a Girl* in *The Shape of a Girl & Jewel* (Vancouver: Talonbooks, 2002), 33, 34.

I walked slowly over the broken glass
And the broken glass couldn't cut my feet because I had no feet
And I didn't bleed as I walked down the sidewalk
And I wasn't crying as I stumbled out into the field
Past all my classmates by the fire and the couch and the cars
Music playing but no one dancing
Just everyone watching
Staring
Quiet at first
And then someone started laughing*

Djanet Sears allows Rainey a moment to herself in her play *The Adventures of a Black Girl in Search of God*. Listen to the rhythms roll out as Rainey details the discovery of her child's death.

**RAINEY:** She's gone. They tell you she's gone. She's in my arms, I'm looking at her and and where's she gone. She's in my arms. I see her little copper feet, I see her tiny fingers, her neck, her lips . . . I know I'm looking at her. And I know . . . I know she's not there. And I'm, I'm, I'm . . . I'm wondering where she went. And you feel . . . I feel . . .

*RAINEY looks up at the sky, trying to dam a stream of tears flooding up inside her.*

Ten billion trillion stars in the universe. Ten billion trillion stars. That's not even counting the planets revolving around them. But it's mostly dark matter. It's 99% empty. One huge vast realm of nothingness.**

Try it yourself. Construct a scene in which only one character speaks. As with any scene, it should feature desire and conflict. Ensure that you know who your character is addressing. Herself? God? Someone that can't be seen? Someone from their memory?

---

* Jordan Tannahill, *Concord Floral* (Toronto: Playwrights Canada Press, 2016), 128-29
** Sears, *The Adventures of a Black Girl in Search of God*, 21.

Be clear in your own mind why they are speaking aloud and what they are doing to get what they want.

POINTS OF ATTENTION

1. Consider what you learn from staying with one character for this length of time.

2. What kind of detail have you discovered about this character's life? What kind of detail about how this person uses language?

3. Consider the kinds of obstacles that a person encounters even when pursuing a goal in isolation.

# EXERCISE EIGHT— SWITCHING SIDES

It's not uncommon to discover that you have presented your protagonist with all the ammunition and your antagonist with none. The play ends up feeling emotionally flat and predictable because the opposing forces seem so clearly overwhelmed in every way, and consequently it becomes impossible for the play to muster any dramatic tension.

For this exercise, try activating the antagonist. Select a scene and rewrite it from the exact opposite impulse. Adopt the perspective of your antagonist and allow this character to launch powerful initiatives and drive the action.

This can prove extremely helpful in terms of generating a more dynamic story and a more vigorous and robust antagonist. Curiously, it may draw your protagonist into sharper focus as well.

Consider the searing volatility of Violet Westin in Tracy Letts's *August: Osage County*, or the relentless machinations of Roy Cohn in Tony Kushner's *Angels in America*. These characters embody forces of antagonism and at the same time shape the dramatic narrative and capture the audience's attention every bit as much as the protagonists. It is precisely because they are forceful, charismatic, and dangerous that the essential conflicts of the play can produce such heat and dynamism.

POINTS OF ATTENTION

1. Fully commit. For a moment, forget that your protagonist is your protagonist, and instead endow your antagonist with the moral weight and stature that you might a protagonist. It's been said that everyone views themselves as the hero of their life. How might this character justify their actions to themselves? What positive attributes do they endow themselves with? Are they resourceful? Pragmatic? Visionary? Captivating? Adept?

2. What goals does this character manifest in this scene, and what concrete actions can they take to achieve those goals? What surprising and effective strategies might they employ?

3. How thoroughly does this character test the protagonist? How closely does he or she approach the successful realization of their overall objectives? What jeopardy might the antagonist place your protagonist in?

4. Now, return to your original work and apply some of these new findings. Permit your antagonist to truly confront, challenge, and test your protagonist.

# EXERCISE NINE—
# TAKE STOCK

An environment needn't be a passive backdrop to action. Instead, try viewing it as a dynamic partner. One way of generating narrative is to closely examine how the characters of your play might interact with their environment. Samuel Beckett is a master of this kind of engagement. In *Endgame*, as the lights rise, the audience views a stark setting featuring two small windows, a door, an armchair covered by a sheet, and a couple of ash bins. The sheet on the armchair, once removed, exposes the brooding, irritable Hamm. Later the ashcans pop open and the venerable Nagg and Nell suddenly emerge to request food, love, or information about the future. In his play *Happy Days*, the central character finds herself in the first act imbedded up to her waist in the earth. In the second act, things escalate and she is embedded up to her neck. The set becomes a genuine agent of antagonism as she struggles with it, attempts to explore her surroundings, and communicate with her husband, who is also immersed in the mound. What potential exists unexplored in your setting? How, by investigating the environment of your story, might you uncover and unlock action and conflict?

POINTS OF ATTENTION

1. Account for all the props and set pieces on stage. Consider the potential they each possess. How might they be employed beyond their most

obvious function? In Sam Shepherd's play *True West*, golf clubs, whiskey bottles, dish towels, and, above all, toasters become objects of competition and aggression between two brothers. How might the most innocent props or conventional setting of your play serve the actors in an unusual or arresting fashion to upset the status quo? To achieve a goal?

2. Consider the materials that might be hidden. What might be discovered in the setting that is not immediately obvious, and when? What might that discovery trigger? In the second act of *Happy Days*, Winnie's husband, long absent, perhaps dead, is summoned many times to no effect, and then unexpectedly emerges from a hole in the debris at the conclusion of the play.

In *The Importance of Being Earnest*, a critical scene turns on the introduction and consumption of a tray of cucumber sandwiches. In Eugène Ionesco's *The Chairs*, the central action of the play involves carrying in and arranging chairs in preparation for a special presentation that is never delivered. And, of course, in *Hamlet*, the prince of Denmark comes across the skull of Yorick, his beloved jester, in a graveyard, the discovery of which spurs him to deliver one of the most celebrated monologues in theatrical history. Allow the materials and setting of your play to influence and incite action in your dramatic works.

# EXERCISE TEN—
# THE REMARKABLE
# PROPERTIES
# OF STUPIDITY

Imagine you are on one side of a very high, very forbidding stone wall. There's a massive iron door in the wall that is locked. You don't have the key and you can't break the door down, yet you must get to someone on the other side. It's urgent. How do you do it?

Take a moment to write down a couple of your stupider solutions—only your least competent, bottom drawer, absolutely demented solutions.

I have given this exercise to students, or exercises of a similar sort. Sometimes I frame it around a particular question involving **plot** or **structure**. I generally deliver it in two parts. First I ask the students to generate those solutions that they believe are workable. In responding to this question, the students often seem stymied. Ideas appear slowly and hesitantly, and only after great effort. Frequently these ideas are accompanied by feelings of dread, uncertainty, and discomfort.

As an example of this, after the requisite time provided to generate an answer had elapsed in class some years back, one nervous student had generated a single solution to the question posed at the top of this page. He had written in very small letters, "Climb the wall."

However, once I have moved on to the second part, and asked for only stupid answers, the responses I receive are most often very different. The answers appear more quickly, more easily, and are offered up more happily. These differences in response are quite striking and are related, I believe, to the failure that is implied within the request, because a stupid response can be equated with a failed response. It is stupid and therefore has failed. It failed *because* it is stupid. It is unworkable. It is unusable. And when I ask for a stupid response from students, I am simply giving them permission to fail.

Some of the responses I have received in the past have been. "Yell and scream and cry until you disintegrate the wall with your tears." "Perform a glacier dance until a glacier sweeps through." "Befriend giant birds." "Build a giant tower of dirt and jump over." "Dig a tunnel under." "Create a flying machine to carry you over."

Let's examine some of the distinctions that are significant in these responses.

1. The speed with which the stupid list is put together. If creating a genuine list takes forever, the stupid list takes next to no time at all. The students can create quite a long list in a very short time.

2. The emotional response to the stupid list is quite different when compared to the "practical" list. The students smile, often laugh, demonstrate feelings of ease, as opposed to groans, moans, grimaces, and other similar resemblances to suffering from a toothache.

3. The final sensation after reading the lists aloud is that the stupid list is not so stupid after all. Some of the answers are obvious. Some of the answers are remarkably creative. Some of the answers are, surprisingly, exactly the same ones that other students have placed on the not-so-stupid list. Some of the answers are far-fetched. Many of the answers are entirely workable.

In striving to be sensible or clever and denying ourselves access to so-called stupid ideas, we may simply be ruling out ideas that seem foreign or uncomfortable—and by extension we may be cutting off access to ideas that are constructive, useful, and genuinely fresh.

And one should point out that the history of theatre, and the history of storytelling in general, is littered with any number of famous and genuinely stupid solutions.

Cyrano, hiding behind Christian in the dark and speaking to Roxane in the guise of Christian, is a highly unlikely, completely demented solution. Oedipus's impassioned solution to the incontrovertible evidence of his complicity in incest and murder is bloody, tragic, and stupid. And, of course, Romeo and Juliet's solution to their marital difficulties complete with faked death and false poison is unspeakably stupid—and at the same time terribly effective.

# EXERCISE ELEVEN—
# THE TEN-MINUTE PLAY

One would never urge a young, untrained athlete to compete in a marathon without first training them to run shorter distances. I have witnessed the theatrical equivalent in playwriting classes where young students are encouraged to move directly from executing simple writing exercises to completing a full-length project. It is incredibly difficult to write and sustain something as long and complicated as a full-length play, or even a longish one-act. Students who try too soon often end up lost in a narrative maze. They struggle, tire, become guilt-ridden and despondent (see my section on failure) beat themselves up over their self-perceived lack of talent, and sometimes abandon writing.

Now, that may be a good thing. Not everyone is going to be a writer. Writing can be a nuisance, and there are many other worthy activities to pursue.

But if encouraging playwriting is the goal, an easier and more effective way to approach things might be to allow students to first work on what is now known as short shorts. A short short is a play meant to be performed in less than fifteen minutes.

The premise behind assigning someone to work on a project of this size is that through attempting to construct and present an entire story in a compressed period of time the writer will begin to develop narrative muscles that can be harnessed later on when they pursue longer and more complex stories.

The fifteen-minute play is a little different from a scene in that it should be a complete and self-contained narrative. All the essential questions raised early in the scene should be answered by the time the lights dim. The piece shouldn't be based upon a previous scene, nor should it anticipate a subsequent scene. There should also be a sense of scale that attends the short short that creates the belief that it is a truly singular moment.

The following short shorts, entitled *Hum* and *Helen at Risk* are two very different examples of this form.

# STUDY ONE—*HUM*
# BY CLEM MARTINI

## Characters

Ann Driscol—a patient
Dr. William Gessler—a neurosurgeon

> *Neurosurgeon Dr. William* GESSLER *readies himself for surgery.* ANN *Driscol, his patient, lies upon an operating table. In the background we hear the bustle and noise associated with the preparation for surgery.*

**ANN:** Dr. Gessler?

GESSLER *continues readying himself.*

**GESSLER:** Yes.

**ANN:** I'm experiencing anxiety.

*He continues readying himself.*

**GESSLER:** Entirely understandable.

**ANN:** I keep thinking that this is an unnatural act.

Then I realize it *is* an unnatural act. It's the most unnatural act I will ever go through. Having the top of my skull cracked, the skin peeled back, the bone lifted like the hood of a car. Having strangers stand about and stare into me. Literally, *into* me.

**GESSLER:** That's fine. Keep talking about it. Feel free to talk about anything you like.

**ANN:** *Me,* talking through it. So *you'll* know if I'm suddenly rendered unable to talk.

All entirely. Unnatural.

**GESSLER:** It's going to be fine.

**ANN:** Don't say that unless you know for sure.

*Beat.*

Could you hum something?

**GESSLER:** Now?

**ANN:** Yes, please.

*Beat.*

It doesn't have to be complicated.

*Beat.*

**GESSLER:** I'm drawing a blank.

**ANN:** It can be anything at all. A lullaby. Anything.

Doctor?

**GESSLER:** *(in a lower voice)* I can't hum.

**ANN:** Pardon me?

**GESSLER:** *(slightly louder)* I can't. Hum.

**ANN:** Try. I need you to try.

**GESSLER:** *(lowering his voice)* I'd rather not.

**ANN:** Just try.

**GESSLER:** Not now.

**ANN:** Please.

**GESSLER:** No.

**ANN:** Then. Stop.

**GESSLER:** What do you mean?

**ANN:** I mean stop. Stop. Everyone, stop.

Until I hear you hum.

>  *Beat.*

**GESSLER:** Can I have the room cleared, please?

>  *A hush falls over the room as it is vacated. Silence.* GESSLER *and* ANN
>  *are left alone.*

What's going on?

**ANN:** Hum.

**GESSLER:** Don't ask me to do this.

**ANN:** But I am, asking.

**GESSLER:** It's like this.

My inability to . . . hum was the cause of considerable, hurtful, scarring humiliation when I was younger. I am, completely, incapable of humming even the smallest musical phrase. Asking me to hum would be like asking a jellyfish to knit a sweater.

**ANN:** I'll have to teach you.

**GESSLER:** You mean now?

**ANN:** Yes.

**GESSLER:** No, I mean. I mean, I'm afraid that won't be possible. I mean, it won't be possible. I mean that's out of the question. I mean, it's not like others haven't tried in the first place. And we can't delay this operation. It's critical to your health. It's essential. And the room is needed immediately after. There are many other operations booked into it. It's like an airport, as one plane is leaving there are others taxiing onto the runway. It's—

**ANN:** I know all that.

**GESSLER:** So there's no time.

**ANN:** There's all the time in the world. All the time in my world. I *know* the risks of this operation.

**GESSLER:** I'm . . . just. I'm afraid what you're asking is impossible. No one can teach me.

The best paid music professionals abandoned the task when I was still quite young.

If you're not talented, in that, that *way*, they pass the information along, you know? They tell each other everything. There's no confidentiality among music teachers. My mother would call people from out of the city and be left with the receiver humming in her hand—they had hung up that quickly. They knew. They'd been warned.

My first, and last, singing coach said I had, how did she put it?—"savaged" that's how she phrased it—"*savaged*" her eardrums. I was ten. I never hummed again.

**ANN:** That's harsh.

**GESSLER:** If I so much as whistled, my mother wept. My father would get visibly irritated. Our dog Skipper ran away and never returned.

I've accepted all this. There are some people who simply cannot hum.

**ANN:** I believe you're wrong.

**GESSLER:** Why is it so critical that I hum for you *now*?

**ANN:** Dr. Gessler, you are entering my brain. My God, my *brain*. The temple of my body, so to speak. Now, I'm a musician. Music is all I know, it is the way I understand the world, it's my sight, my smell, my touch, my taste, my thought, my soul, it is everything to me. How can I trust you to rearrange the alignment of the most vital part of me if you can't connect with me on this most elemental level?

Let me teach you to hum.

**GESSLER:** Ah, no.

**ANN:** Yes.

**GESSLER:** This is a bad time, do you understand? This is the very definition of a bad time; it makes every other time look like a really good time in comparison, it's very, very—

**ANN:** Look. Humming is something that comforts me. I'm nervous. I'm tense. I've fasted for twenty-four hours, so I'm hungry as well. That throws off my blood sugar and makes me cranky and irritable. I'm not naturally belligerent or argumentative or cantankerous, but I don't normally have the top of my skull lifted or metal probes inserted in my brain or have a tumour the size of a walnut removed. So I'm inclined to have my way in this matter. Now nature has seen fit to include humming in the idiom of the animal kingdom—the ruby-throated hummingbird, some species of owl, and even the normally very busy, no-nonsense straight-by-the-books honeybee hums, so to paraphrase the song, birds do it, bees do it, perhaps even surgeons with degrees should do it. It doesn't have to be painful. It doesn't have to take long. *Humour* me.

**GESSLER:** O. Kay. Fine. I'll try.

**ANN:** So what will it be?

**GESSLER:** I have no idea.

**ANN:** What would you choose to hum?

**GESSLER:** I wouldn't even know where to start.

**ANN:** What sort of music do you *enjoy*?

*Beat.*

**GESSLER:** Contemporary,

**ANN:** Contemporary. That's a start. Let's try to draw the focus a little tighter.

Can you think of a title or an artist?

*Beat.*

**GESSLER:** Billy. Joel?

**ANN:** Billy Joel? All right. I can work with that. Breathe in. Exhale. Feel your throat vibrate.

*He breathes.*

You'll have to allow it to make a sound.

**GESSLER:** I'm hyperventilating.

**ANN:** It's fine. Breathe. Slowly. Breathe.

You have to put yourself back in sync with the music of the spheres.

**GESSLER:** I suppose.

**ANN:** Keep breathing.

**GESSLER:** Of course . . .

**ANN:** What?

**GESSLER:** Well. It's just that. There *is* no music of the spheres. There are no spheres. That's strictly remnant terminology.

**ANN:** "Remnant terminology." What's that mean?

**GESSLER:** It's a completely discredited way of thinking. It dates back to Aristotelian philosophy prior to a solar-centric model of the universe.

**ANN:** Can you just talk?

**GESSLER:** There are *no spheres* is what I'm saying.

**ANN:** Of course there are spheres.

**GESSLER:** Where?

**ANN:** Not spheres you can *see*, necessarily, and they're not anything you can touch or hold in the palm of your hand, but they exist. Spheres of space and time, spheres of influence, spheres of the human heart and soul, and the vibrations they emit, I'm telling you, they are shimmying up and through you right now.

Water flowing over rocks and into pools generates its own cascading musical composition. In the desert, prevailing winds arc across dunes producing something like harmony. Can you honestly believe with solar winds sweeping through the vast expanse of the universe, through quarks and quasars, molecules and space debris, dark matter and subatomic particles that there is no music?

Feel it.

**GESSLER:** I can't. I'm sorry.

**ANN:** Close your eyes.

**GESSLER:** I make it a rule never to close my eyes while in the operating room.

**ANN:** But you're not in the operating room right now. You're somewhere else. Close your eyes.

**GESSLER:** But—

**ANN:** Sh. Close them.

*He does.*

There.

You're sitting on the porch at the very edge of the world.

You're looking over the edge and can see everything dropping away at your feet. The cosmos. The stars. Nebulas expanding. Black holes contracting. And there's a faint, insistent, compelling rhythm like the far-off howling of coyotes sweeping up from this void. And if you sit very still you will hear that sound, feel the urgency of it surge through your spine and the force of it blow your hair back.

Listen.

**GESSLER:** I'm listening.

**ANN:** Are you?

**GESSLER:** I am.

**ANN:** Can you hear it?

*Beat.*

**GESSLER:** Yes.

**ANN:** There's nothing there but ... that sound ... your voice, and you.

Breathe in. Breathe out. Now hum.

**GESSLER:** Will you hold my hand?

*They hold hands and begin to hum. A Billy Joel tune, as it turns out.*

**ANN:** That's not so bad.

*They hum a moment longer.*

So, let's recap.

You're going to enter through the top of my skull, penetrate my frontal lobe, and remove tissue from Wernicke's area in the left hemisphere.

**GESSLER:** Yes.

**ANN:** And it's likely that I'll experience . . . some hearing loss after?

**GESSLER:** The way the foreign tissue is placed, I'd say that's a probability. Yes.

**ANN:** Then I would prefer it if you continued humming, please.

**GESSLER:** We'll hum together.

Are you ready?

**ANN:** I am completely ready.

**GESSLER:** Can I have everyone back in now?

*The rest of the crew re-enters and the sound of preparations begins once again.*

**ANN:** Keep humming.

*Lights narrow to a single spot on* ANN.

Keep humming.

Keep humming.

*Music rises—music by Billy Joel, of course. The lights slowly fade to black.*

*The end.*

# STUDY TWO—*HELEN AT RISK*
# BY DANA YEATON

## Characters

Helen—an attractive middle-aged woman, dressed sensibly but with an artistic flair.
Ronnie Guyette—an inmate.
Guard

## Time and Place

A prison rec room.

*A long table centre stage; downstage and to one side, a chair.*

*At rise:* RONNIE *is lying on the table, a kerchief covering his hair, while* HELEN *applies the final touches to his white plaster mask.* GUARD *sits facing audience.*

**HELEN:** *(to audience)* Now this last piece, the little triangular, Vermont piece, or . . .

*Turns it upside down.*

New Hampshire–shaped piece, depending . . .

*She dunks it in a small Tupperware container of murky white water. Throughout the play, she continues to shape and smooth the mask with her hands.*

This will go between the nostrils, not over the nostrils, or your partner will no longer be able to breathe. Now in your kits you will find that I have pre-cut all the pieces which I do not like to do but I had all I could do to get plaster and paint supplies in here and they definitely were not going to let me hand out scissors. So now really, I'm just smoothing, the forehead's already hard, of course the nose will be the last to dry. *Do not hurry the mask,* it should be completely hard before you try to take it off. I will show you how to do that in a minute—

*(to man whose mask she is making)* How ya doin' there, Ronnie? Happy? No complaints, right? Yes it was an education just trying to get in here, the Arts Council had warned us about belts, so I knew to come beltless, and no gum to stick in the locks, I can understand that, but pens? Ballpoint pens? Apparently you boys start tattooing yourself, is that right? . . .

*(responding to an inmate)* No I don't mind tattoos, one of my friends has a lovely little tattoo . . . I'm not tellin' where! You just pay attention to what I'm doing because in a minute *you* are gonna be up here doing the same thing . . . Now doesn't Ronnie look peaceful? And look at those cheekbones . . .

*(to another inmate)* No, you are not allowed to say anything to people who are having their masks done. Especially—

*RONNIE gives the finger.*

Especially . . . this is the time when the slightest little move can . . . good, now the jaws are fully dry and the chin is coming.

*(to GUARD)* How are we doin' for time?

**GUARD:** Nine twenty.

**HELEN:** And we can go till when?

**GUARD:** We got room check at ten.

**HELEN:** Ooh. Okay. That's gonna be a little tight.

*(to GUARD)* Sure you don't wanna join in?

**GUARD:** I'm sure.

**HELEN:** Okay ... *(shrugs)* Well we gotta keep uh, lemme see, why don't I tell you a little bit about what we do once the mask is *dry* ... um ... we may end up cutting some of the decoration time short. What I usually do in the schools is set out two or three tables of materials. Beads, feathers, ribbon, paints, glitter, knick-knacks—I love yard sales—and I ask that you find some colours or objects, any combinations of paints and materials that will make the mask express who *you are.* Now today, as I said, we're going to use—I was only allowed three brushes, so we're going to have to share. I'm not quite clear on what the danger of a paintbrush is but .... What have we got here?

*(inspecting another Tupperware container, full of paints)* Black, blue, um yellow, peach, I hope y'all won't use a lot of the peach, though I don't actually ...

I don't see my red. Pardon? ...

*(to an inmate)* Well no, you can use the peach, I just think, you know, I want to encourage you to experiment, use your imagination and not feel like your mask has to be the same colour as you ... though I can see that, well we, if you would LIKE to use black, some of you, or anybody, that's up to you. We're looking for something that expresses *you,* how you feel as a person, how you feel today, right now.

**GUARD:** *(in response to an inmate)* Pearson!

**HELEN:** *(to GUARD)* No that's okay.

*(to Pearson)* If that's how you really feel then try to imagine how that shapes your face and let that be the mask and later before you do any decorating—we're all dry through here now *(re: chin)*, we're just waiting on the nose—before you paint or do anything, make sure that you have an image in your mind, in your mind's eye, of what your mask should finally be ... Yes I suppose you could. Sure, sort

of a fantasy of what you'd like to be. That would be equally valid. Now we just keep—

*RONNIE is pretending to masturbate.*

**GUARD:** *(to RONNIE)* Guyette!

**HELEN:** *(placing RONNIE's hand at his side)* We'll just put this over here . . . Ronnie doesn't seem to understand how simple it would be for us to place another piece of plaster right along here.

*(pretending to cover the nose completely)* I should tell you that for some people having your eyes completely covered can be very . . . disorienting, very frightening. A man once, I was out in Colorado, at this convention, and this man had volunteered to be the guinea pig, he was very excited about the idea, and about ten minutes into the demonstration—

*RONNIE bolts upright, shaking as if terrified.*

*(pulling him down to flat again)* DO NOT MOVE until the mask is off or you will—

**GUARD:** Guyette, you're gonna be outta here.

**HELEN:** Ronnie will be good, won't you, Ronnie? . . . There now, lie back . . .

Good. For some reason the nose always takes the longest to dry . . .

*(to Pearson)* Yes I am. Are you?

**GUARD:** Pearson! . . . Yeah, I heard what you asked.

**HELEN:** I don't like to wear my ring when I'm working with plaster.

242

**GUARD:** Look, these guys don't have to be in here. Anybody you want out, say so.

**HELEN:** We're fine. Look, I appreciate, I mean *(laughs)* for God's sake, I have worked in junior high schools!

**GUARD:** Okay.

**HELEN:** *Then* it would have been nice to have a guard.

**GUARD:** Your call.

**HELEN:** If I need you I can always just scream, right?

**GUARD:** Whatever.

**HELEN:** Y'all promise to be good, don't you?

*(in response to Pearson)* I'll bet you are. Um . . . one thing we *may* want to do since we will be a little short on time is use *warm* water for soaking because this will speed the drying process; *however* warm water *will* mean that we have to work a little faster to keep it from setting before we're . . .

*(to Pearson)* Pardon? . . . You mean today? . . . I just thought it would be fun . . . Well, *that* and I think it's important for people to learn more about who— Yes. I am . . . . Well I'd rather not . . . A hundred and fifty dollars, not including the materials, which of course here don't really amount— Because that's *not* why I'm here. If I wanted to make money I'd go do that. I think people deserve a chance to—this always sounds stupid but I *do* think there is a basic human need to create and to express yourself. See, you think I'm an outsider, I don't think I'm an outsider.

Whatever happened to you *before*, what your parents did, I don't know the particulars but . . . I mean I think I know what it's like to grow up with no one caring what you think or feel. You're just some piece of furniture. And finally you blow up, of course! Thank God. You're alive! Do you ever look at other people and really think about being *them*? Which would mean everything about them, their families, their genes, every experience, but you're still *you*, you still know that you're only visiting. There was a little boy, maybe one of yours, waiting to get buzzed out while I was waiting to get buzzed in, and his mother was doing something at the front desk and through the glass, he couldn't see me I guess or didn't care, but he was opening, he seemed to be practising opening his mouth as wide as he could. And he wasn't saying anything, but I could see way back in his throat.

RONNIE *taps her arm.*

Oops, I think our guinea pig is telling us it's time.

*(to Pearson)* And by the way, I *do* need the money.

*(touching the mask)* Okay, does it feel hard all over?

RONNIE *does a spectacular mock orgasm.*

That is not what I—

*(trying to restrain him)* I can see I have to be careful what I say to *this* man. Now stay still. STOP! . . . There.

*(to GUARD)* See how well he minds?

*(to all)* Now, what I *was* going to say is that when you are having your mask made, you'll notice how as the plaster hardens it cools. So you should be able to tell *from the inside* when it's ready to come off. Now I want to demonstrate how we remove the mask. You in the back, make sure you can see this. First you v-e-e-ry gently slip your fingers up under here *(re: the cheeks)* and you just keep working your way around, under the chin. Careful not to pinch. Nice and gentle. You should feel it coming loose. All right, see how it starts to come away,

and we . . . this is where you find out if you used enough Vaseline. Ready? . . . Voila.

*The mask is off.* RONNIE *sits up, bits of plaster on his face. He pulls off the kerchief.*

*(handing mask to* RONNIE*)* And that, my friend . . . is you.

RONNIE *stares, unimpressed.*

Most people have only a two-dimensional image of themselves, which is what a mirror gives you or a photo. But. Here . . .

HELEN *turns the mask to show* RONNIE *its profile.*

What you're looking at right now, maybe for the first time ever, is your third dimension . . . Now before you say anything, here's your paint-brush. Kinda big but do your best— Oh first we need to get your name written on the inside so we don't get 'em confused. Don't want any arguments over whose face is whose . . . Course, I don't have a pen.

GUARD: *(pulling a pen from his pocket)* I can do it.

HELEN: Great. You don't mind?

GUARD: *(to* RONNIE*)* C'm'ere.

RONNIE *crosses, hands mask to* GUARD, *who writes in it.*

HELEN: See, I knew we'd get him participating. Now before we all get started, I just want to remind you that with the Vaseline, do a good, thorough job, remember that beards and moustaches will have to be covered with *tissue* paper, and make sure to go way up into the hairline. There's no such thing as—

RONNIE: *(to* GUARD*)* Try it on.

**GUARD:** No.

**RONNIE:** Come on. Just try it.

*(to inmates)* Don't ya think he should try it on?

*(after an enthusiastic "yeah")* All right. Let's see.

*GUARD holds mask to his face.*

*RONNIE looks to the inmates, then turns and drives the large wooden paintbrush deep into the eye of the mask. He slashes side to side. GUARD falls to the floor, thrashes for a moment, then lies still.*

*RONNIE pulls the mask from the GUARD's face. He uses the paintbrush to wipe blood from the back of the mask, then flips it and paints a trail of blood descending, like a tear, from the eye hole.*

Hey, look.

*(holding the mask out to HELEN)* It's me.

*They stand facing each other, motionless.*

Aren't ya gonna try it on?

*Beat.*

*Blackout.*

*End.*

The short short compels one to make hard decisions about selection and distillation. At the same time it holds the ability to say big things and make bold statements in a very compressed time. These two brief works provide examples of the kind of scope and variety that can be tackled in very few pages.

What began some decades back as a novelty has evolved into a form practised and enjoyed across the continent. Part of the thrill that accompanies working in this shortest of play forms lies in embracing its economy and precision.

A short short won't allow you to write your opus or chronicle all of civilization. But it will allow you to learn exactly what can be accomplished in ten to fifteen minutes. And, in the end, what is a full-length play but a larger play constructed of a string of ten- to fifteen-minute stretches? Learn to deal with ten minutes effectively and efficiently and eventually you'll be able to accomplish whatever you wish with one hundred and ten.

# WILL PERFORMING THESE WRITING EXERCISES MAKE ME A BETTER PLAYWRIGHT?

In general, any kind of sustained writing activity will lead to improved writing ability, but I suppose the postscript to that is that improvement can only occur if you first permit the writing to change you.

To improve as a playwright, you must open yourself—to the things you may learn from the writing, to the critiques you receive from others, to the possibility of improvement.

These exercises will allow you—if you are open to the experience—to add new tools to your tool kit, that's all. Ultimately, what you construct with the tool kit is your call.

# PART NINE
## BUSINESS SENSE AND
## PARTING THOUGHTS

# WORKSHOPS, DEVELOPMENT, AND DRAMATURGY

Following the completion of a draft, playwrights are often moved to seek dramaturgical assistance.

The term *dramaturgy* was first coined in the European arena. It referred to a process within a play's production that provided research and contextual material to the director and cast. It was meant to assist in the understanding of a particular text. A dramaturge was an individual who aided the director by providing research that illuminated some aspect of the text in production, and allowed the text to be more accurately and effectively presented.

Over the last five decades, however, a new kind of dramaturgy has evolved that is more focused on the development of new work. In this model, a dramaturge is someone whose alliance lies primarily with the playwright. These dramaturges become familiar with the emerging text and attempt to shed light on both the strengths and weaknesses of the developing work so that the playwright may view the text for what it truly is and develop a plan to shape and edit the play accordingly.

Dramaturges may assist individually with playwrights, or they may serve in the context of a workshop.

A workshop is a collective endeavour that many theatres employ to provide useful analysis of developing plays and so support playwrights.

These workshops can take many forms. Some are short, intense periods of discussion and examination of only a day. Some of the workshops extend over several days and engage the efforts and scrutiny of a director and an assembled cast. Other workshops are more elaborate affairs involving a series of guided explorations that transpire over a period of months or even years, and may draw upon the talents of designers, actors, and composers.

Workshops, and the dramaturgy associated with workshops, can be extremely useful. Because theatre is so collaborative a venture, it can be helpful to the playwright to draw upon the talents of others. There may be structural difficulties that were previously hidden from the playwright that become apparent after discussion with a dramaturge. A conversation with a designer may allow you to better understand a play's visual potential.

A word of caution, however. There is no degree, diploma, or certificate required to confer a person with the title of "consultant." The same is true of a dramaturge. Anyone who is so inclined can hang out their shingle, and dramaturgy is only ever as good as the person delivering it. Before you decide to workshop your play, do your research. Examine the track record of the organization and individuals involved. Solicit advice from other playwrights who have worked with this dramaturge.

If you do decide to have your material workshopped:

1. Don't bring a script to a workshop until you feel that it's ready. Know what you hope to get from the workshop.

2. Talk with the person directing the workshop. Discuss your goals with the director of the workshop before it commences.

3. Remember that the process is an exploration, not an interrogation—and if you feel the company is confused on this point, remind *them*.

# SENDING IT OFF

When you feel the script has been revised sufficiently and is complete and production-ready, the next step should be to perform some final research. Where are you going to send your play?

First, ask yourself what audience the script is intended to reach. Is your play an edgy, in-your-face drama laced with profanity? Great!—but it's not likely that it will receive a friendly read from your family-oriented summer stock theatre. Don't waste your time—or theirs.

There are a number of Internet resources that will be of assistance as you try to determine where you should direct your play. The Professional Association of Canadian Theatres and Theatre Communications Group websites are useful spots to start, or perform more specific searches and make a list of the theatres that appear to be likely candidates.

Look for submission guidelines on theatre websites, or phone or email to learn how the theatre wishes to be approached. Some theatres prefer to receive queries first. This involves crafting a letter introducing yourself and describing your play in succinct but compelling terms. Don't allow the letter to run to more than a couple of pages. Sometimes an additional short sample of the script is requested. If the theatre's literary manager is interested in your query you may then be invited to send your script along.

Other theatres prefer to receive and review the script in its entirety right away. Most theatres prefer that scripts be sent electronically, although some still prefer hard copies. When mailing a theatre your script, the usual procedure is to prepare two envelopes, one addressed to yourself, and one to the theatre. Affix sufficient postage on both. Place the self-addressed envelope within the envelope addressed to the theatre, along with your script, and a brief letter of introduction. Seal the envelope, whisper a little prayer, and send the package along its way.

Whether sent electronically or mailed, don't expect a quick response. Theatres tend to be overworked, under-funded, and chronically behind in their reading; and although resources often list the turnaround time as something like four to six weeks, it's best to lower your expectations. If you haven't heard from a theatre in six months, you can try sending a gentle nudge. And always comply with the submission directions supplied by the theatre—nothing is more likely to get your play rejected than assuming that you alone may ignore their guidelines.

# ON PRIZES, AWARDS, AND COMPETITIONS

As a person entering the craft, submitting plays to writing competitions is one very good way of gaining recognition, publicity, and, occasionally, remuneration. There are many legitimate and important contests out there, both locally and internationally, but be careful about which ones you enter. In this, as in all things, caution is required, and it is important that you first do your homework. Find out who operates the contest. Be suspicious of competitions with large entry fees. Check to be absolutely certain that the contests are legitimately operated and have successfully distributed their prizes in the past. Determine precisely what the nature of the prize is. A contest whose only prize is written commentary and an assurance to refer your work to some supposedly important but unnamed agencies at some unspecified time in the future should be avoided.

# REHEARSAL

Rehearsals can be very instructive, and I would encourage playwrights to attend them wherever possible. This is especially true when it comes to premieres. The rehearsal represents a golden opportunity to continue the exploration of your play, and allows you to make further discoveries and apply final edits and alterations.

It's important to realize that as the play nears opening, you must be prepared to turn the play over to other participants in this collaborative process, however. That collaborative process has a protocol that you must respect, and part of that protocol involves learning how to deliver your notes and critique.

The accepted procedure for delivering acting notes, or notes of any kind, is to deliver them to the director. The director then either passes the notes along or incorporates them into their own and passes them along. That way, the actor, or the costumer, or the lighting designer won't become confused by receiving two conflicting directions.

# ON REVIEWS

Reviews are an inevitable part of the theatre.

So long as plays are produced there will be folks who write commentary, and today with the proliferation of Internet blogs, email postings, and articles, there has never been a greater opportunity for the ill-informed to find arenas to log their poorly considered opinion pieces.

At their very best, reviews may offer insights and observations that genuinely illuminate a production—and draw an audience. At their worst, reviews can be sloppy, arbitrary, cruel, and wrong. Either way, there is little the playwright can do except to write the play to the best of their ability. If you want to stay sane *and* write plays you will have to find a way to deal with both positive and negative reviews.

If you can glean anything useful from them, do so. Otherwise, best to ignore them.

# SELF-PRODUCTION

As the costs associated with producing theatre have risen, getting the unusual and the idiosyncratic script produced has become more and more problematic. Some decades back, Fringe festivals arose in response to this kind of systemic, implicit censorship. A worldwide phenomenon, the Fringe festivals that sprang up were devoted to the odd and eccentric, the stories that for any one of many reasons could not find their way onto the stages of the larger theatres.

Then the Fringe itself matured and evolved, and as a result of its own success became a bit of a conventional convention, with its own set of standard practices and normalized expectations. Now, there are more and more writers who, not finding a ready market available in the mainstream or the Fringe, have decided to produce their own works.

These self-produced works most often operate within limited budgets, may be site-specific, and are aimed at a very select market. A good percentage of these works are solo performances.

Self-production may provide you with a mechanism to put your play before an audience, and it may do even more than that. It may allow you to endow it with the kind of careful, attentive production that only you can envision or provide. But it can be tiring. What it saves in cash, it costs in energy and attention to detail, and it will consume your time like nothing else.

For all that, self-production can be empowering because it provides the playwright with options. If you feel so inclined, have the necessary skills, and are prepared for the heavy workload and responsibility, it can present a bracing alternative to the standard protocol of "writing, emailing, and waiting."

# ON COLLABORATION

All theatre is a cross-disciplinary exercise that requires the efforts of visual artists, actors, designers, and a number of individuals whose primary discipline is bossiness.

Some theatrical works are a tad more collaborative than others, however.

There is a growing movement of writers who have discovered that there is tremendous energy and invention to be tapped by working through the complications and quandaries of narrative with others.

Collectives can be exciting enterprises, and one of their great strengths is that they can incorporate the gifts and talents of a variety of people. There can be difficulties that arise out of collaborative situations, however, and these difficulties generally arise when the individuals involved attempt to resolve a fair method of compensation and recognition for the work involved.

If everyone's involvement in a collaborative situation could be said to be equal, then perhaps there would be no problem, but most often that's not the case. Sometimes everyone provides suggestions for scenes or dialogue, and one person writes out a script. Sometimes individuals improvise scenes, which may be used, but equally may not be. Sometimes one person becomes the designated writer for one draft, and another becomes the designated writer for another draft.

How to determine a fair method of compensation when the efforts put into generating the script are so hard to calculate? What happens when one person wrote nothing, improvised nothing, but generated the initial idea that the play is based upon? These problems are complicated if the play goes on to be performed by other groups in other theatres.

As Chair of Contracts at the Playwrights Guild I've had to act as an intervener in a number of conflicts that arose out of these kinds of situations. Most often the playwright would say something like, "I've just finished writing a draft. I was given some money to hold me over while I wrote, but now that I've finished the draft they say they owe me nothing for all the work I did." I would then ask if they were working from a contract, and after a short, embarrassed silence, they would tell me no.

In cases such as these, I might be able to exert some moral pressure on the group and attempt to embarrass them into paying the playwright— but if there isn't a contract, there isn't much that can legally be done.

Now, here's the thing. Sometimes the playwrights found in situations like this were the victims of unscrupulous individuals, but most often that hasn't been the case. Most often the problem has resulted from poor communication. The individuals involved simply hadn't taken the time to discuss what they truly envisioned to be the nature of their involvement.

The best advice that one can give to anyone working in a collaborative environment is to draft a letter of agreement before you enter into the exercise. Be clear about what is expected of each individual, be clear about each participant's level of involvement, and be clear how each person expects to be compensated. The conversation you convene early on may be a difficult one, but it's sure to be easier than a litigious conversation later.

# ON PUBLICATION

Because plays were traditionally meant to be viewed in production rather than read, publication of a text isn't usually invested with the same importance or urgency that it possesses in other literary forms. There are, after all, relatively few people who purchase plays for the pure pleasure of reading them.

If a play is going to be published it generally must be preceded by a successful production history. That's not always the case, however. There are magazines, for instance, that cater to specific audience interests, and these magazines and journals sometimes accept unproduced plays. It's best to do an Internet search to see if your play fits into one of these particular niches.

Though production is the acknowledged primary goal of the playwright, there is tremendous value in having your play published. Publication provides the play with a longer shelf life—literally—and it can expose your play to potential producers outside the arena you might have otherwise considered and consequently generate new productions.

# THE BUSINESS OF
# WRITING

"Be professional."

This is advice I hear delivered to playwrights all the time. "Be professional."

I hesitate to give it because I don't know what it means. It makes playwriting sound like a profession and I'm not sure it is. If a profession is something that involves getting up in the morning, going off to work, putting in your hours of labour, and receiving a paycheque at the end of the week, playwriting is certainly not that. If it's about developing a product and marketing and receiving financial rewards for good salesmanship, well . . . playwriting's not exactly that either. There is plenty about playwriting that is irregular, irreverent, iconoclastic, and, quite frankly, unprofessional, and there are times when I think playwriting more closely resembles mysticism than it does a profession.

By "being professional" I suppose what is meant is that one should approach their discipline with rigour, accept that there is a protocol that accompanies receiving payment for their work, and that they should try to be honest and forthright in how they approach that aspect of their art. There *are* some individuals practising playwriting who don't accept any protocol, who feel that they are *not* compelled to keep promises or deadlines because they believe they answer to a higher calling, and work to a different set of standards. These individuals belong to a special category that may be called scam artists. They do a disservice to playwriting, and you want to avoid joining their ranks.

I suppose when it comes to the business of playwriting, I would offer the kind of advice you would give almost anyone. Keep your promises. If you accept a deadline for an assignment, meet it. If you are given a commission to complete a work, complete it. Don't take on more creative work than you can reasonably expect to finish. Let every text you complete be an example of your integrity. Proofread your scripts rigorously. Don't submit a script until it is finished to the best of your ability. Always obtain a contract, and before you sign it, read it.

And write for yourself. There are so few guarantees in playwriting. If you write for yourself, you are guaranteed to at least make one person happy, and ultimately I've found that the plays one writes to satisfy and entertain one's self often end up entertaining others as well.

Remember that theatre is an art form comprised of an intricate web of relationships. In a very real sense, there is no play without a production, and there is no production without a director, designer, or actors. If you discover that you work well with someone, if you find someone who understands your work, and whose work you in turn admire, cherish that relationship. It's gold. Good work often evolves out of good relationships. The work of Anton Chekhov evolved out of a relationship with Constantin Stanislavski. The work of Tennessee Williams developed in relationship with Elia Kazan. A sound and solid relationship with someone who understands your work and is able to translate it is a thing of rare worth.

Look after yourself, because no one else will. As a playwright you will inevitably end up exchanging scripts and invoices with organizations that have administrative departments, financial divisions, and excellent legal advice. The only thing that can protect you is to ensure that you have a contract and that the contract is ethical. There are organizations that are designed to support and provide professional advice to playwrights. (I have listed several at the back of the book.) Join one or several. Agents aren't as useful as one might first imagine in terms of procuring work, but they are very effective when it comes to protecting work and negotiating a good rate. Once you have produced a body of work that you feel comfortable showing around, you might consider making an appointment to see an agent about representation.

I've been President of the Playwrights Guild of Canada, and, before that, Contracts Chair. I saw the statistics. There are many dedicated people out there who are writing and only a fraction are able to wring a living wage from their craft. If it's a profession, it's a peculiar one. Some theatres perform new plays, others aren't interested. Some theatres respond promptly to queries, others can't even be bothered to return email. I cannot begin to tell you how many playwrights, and good playwrights who have enjoyed multiple productions and international successes, have thrown up their hands in despair. Writing for the theatre is too difficult, they'll tell you, too arbitrary, too fickle, too frustrating.

But playwriting also holds a thrilling power, and it's addictive. Theatre manages to thrive under the most daunting conditions. When the former Czechoslovakia was struggling under Soviet influence, and the content of theatre was monitored and censored, playwrights continued to write plays critical of the state and performed them secretly in tiny but crowded living rooms for very select, but very passionate, audiences. Was it "professional" to perform to only eight or nine people at a time? Perhaps not, but I'm not really interested in turning playwriting into a business. I'm not sure that it can be turned into a business. I'm more concerned that the human element in this most human art form not be diminished, that plays continue to have the capacity to genuinely move people and shake and shape society.

Be passionate, be committed, dig in, and fight to get your work done with the degree of artistry and care that it requires—and in your business dealings, by all means, be professional.

# ON HOW SOCIETY VIEWS
# ART AND ARTISTS

Society has a problem with playwrights, which, to an extent, it has with all artists.

On the one hand it tends to idealize playwrights. It sees them as engaged in a perpetually pleasant activity that doesn't really require the same kind of rigour or experience that other professions do, nor does it appear to require that they suffer the same kind of daily drudgery that other non-artists are compelled to endure.

Playwrights don't punch clocks. They don't bus to work each day. They don't have to tolerate a bullying, shouting boss. They're not required to wear unflattering uniforms. They don't get their hands dirty, don't clean up after customers, don't work in a toxic environment. They sleep in, wake late, dash off the odd play, then saunter to some party that the public is certain will be populated by a lot of other facile, self-absorbed, shallow, debauched—but happy—artists.

In short, they are playwrights (you may equally fill in the blank with painters, poets, musicians, whatever) because they are very lucky.

On the other hand, society also views playwrights as freeloaders, scammers, and social parasites. In this paradoxical vision, artists complete endless applications for extravagant government grants that, once received, are promptly applied to their prodigious drinking or drug-taking regimens. Playwrights are phoney. They write plays heavily laced with profanity and gratuitous sexuality or are couched in pseudo intellectual jargon to mask the fact that they really have nothing to say. They eke out a meagre living and are only barely better than beggars.

In short, they are playwrights (fill in dancers, sculptors, composers, whatever) because they couldn't get another job.

These are not views developed recently. St. Augustine of Hippo (345–430 CE) proclaimed, "Stage plays are the most petulant, the most impure, impudent, wicked, unclean, the most shameful and detestable atonements of filthy Devil-gods."

Ovid (43 BCE–18 CE) in his *Ars Amatoria* wrote, "Adulterers, Whore-masters, Panders, Whores and such like, effeminate, idle unchaste, lascivious, graceless persons were the most assiduous Play-hunters in their time," vilifying everyone involved in the theatre.

The influence of these two divergent attitudes is manifested in many ways. In the way playwrights are presented in the media. In the kind of attention that plays are given. (I was once informed that a newspaper intentionally assigned someone to review plays who knew nothing about theatre because the editor opined, "Most people don't know anything about plays," and he felt the reviewer should be similarly ignorant. I suppose I could argue that most people know nothing about advanced science and technology, but that particular editor would have been scandalized had I suggested that the reporter assigned to the technology section shouldn't require some kind of background knowledge in science.) Above all, it is manifested in a kind of brooding anger and resentment that is revealed in all kinds of not-so-subtle passive-aggressive comments. When people ask what you *really* do for a living, or when people suggest that now that you have made a living, maybe it's time to begin "giving back to society." (Because of course, all the time that you were writing, you were taking.)

Develop a thick skin and never give in. Remember that playwriting has a long, illustrious, influential history, and art is one of the few things that ever made civilization civilized or society tolerable. Never permit people to marginalize or trivialize your work. Every day that you write, write full-out. Celebrate your art and challenge the notion that playwriting is frivolous, that art is a hobby, that paying attention to story is a self-indulgence.

# ON FAILURE

When *The Seagull* was first performed in 1896 in St. Petersburg, the audience booed, hissed, and walked out. Chekhov left the theatre after that opening night vowing never to write again.

Aristophanes, the individual often referred to as the "father of Greek comedy," endured a humiliating failure when his play *The Clouds* took last place in a festival.

Molière's play, *Tartuffe*, following its initial production, was denounced for seeking to undermine the foundations of religion itself, and prohibited from production in Paris by the king of France.

Giuseppe Verdi, one of the principal figures of opera, was refused entry to study at the musical conservatory in Milan. One of his greatest works, *La Traviata*, was a flop when it first opened.

The first ten years of George Bernard Shaw's career as a playwright, 1891 through 1901, were plagued by failure, with very few productions, or productions characterized by single performances by private societies.

Henrik Ibsen failed the Greek and mathematics portions of his university entrance exam and was refused admittance. In his position as artistic director of the Norske Theatre, the company went bankrupt. His early plays failed to draw an audience until in 1860 he nearly had a nervous breakdown.

Response to his plays was often unimpressive. His play *Rosmersholm* received this commentary from the *Gentlewoman* when it was first performed in London in 1891, "These Ibsen creatures are 'neither men nor women, they are ghouls,' vile, unlovable, unnatural, morbid monsters, and it were well indeed for society if all such went and drowned themselves at once."*

And, of course, it was only after Eugene O'Neill had failed as a gold prospector in Honduras (as a kind of apprenticeship, I would suggest, to prepare for the rigours of his later avocation), that he even decided to give playwriting a try.

Feelings of failure plague the act of playwriting. Nor should one believe that feelings of failure arise only out of failure. A sense of failure can be extracted just as easily from the jaws of success. In Tennessee Williams's introduction to *The Glass Menagerie* he talks about the intense depression he fell into immediately following the success of that play. "I got so sick of hearing people say, 'I love your play!' that I could not say thank you any more. I choked on the words and turned rudely away from the usually sincere person. I no longer felt any pride in the play itself but began to dislike it . . . "

Significantly, however, one of the things that rescued him from this melancholy was writing. "Then, as a final act of restoration, I settled for a while at Chapala to work on a play called *The Poker Night*, which later became *A Streetcar Named Desire*. It is only in this work that an artist can find reality and satisfaction . . . "**

That's often the case. Failure, or the perception of failure, leads to a kind of revisioning, and, ultimately, renewal. It's possible that failure is only one part of a longer cycle that leads back, if you let it, to further creation.

So, maybe failure can be the playwright's friend. Or, if not a friend, then perhaps the annoying uncle who is a little bit mean, a little bit sarcastic, smells of smoke, and says true but hurtful things when he's had too much to drink. After all, failure urges one to adapt. It forces one to consider one's work with a critical eye. It compels one to let go of bad habits.

And besides . . . success isn't necessarily everything it's cracked up to be either. Had Napoleon not been so stunningly successful in his 1796 campaigns at Montenotte and Mondovì he might not have concluded that he was capable of subduing and controlling all of Europe. This fatal early introduction to success and the subsequent imprudent lessons learned by the young Napoleon led to a devastated Europe, the betrayal of the

---

* Diana Rigg, *No Turn Unstoned* (London: Arrow Books, 1987), 127.

** Williams, "The Catastrophe of Success" in *The Glass Menagerie*, 14.

ideals of the French Revolution, and his ultimate exile to the lonely, rocky, windswept isle of Elba, which can't have been good for his health or emotional disposition. Success can dispense lessons every bit as dangerous and deadly as those of failure.

# EXODUS

*You ask how I write my plays. Alas! I would rather tell you how I do not write them.*

*Have you noticed the small number of new writers who take their chances in the theatre? The explanation is that in reality, for our genera- tion of free artists, the theatre is repugnant, with its cookery, its hobbles, its demand for immediate and brutal success, its army of collaborators, to which one must submit, from the imposing leading man down to the prompter.*\*
—Emile Zola

Things haven't changed so very much since the esteemed Mr. Zola penned those words. It's certainly, simultaneously, the best and worst of times.

The percentage of the population that actually attends live theatre is small and continues to decline. It becomes more and more expensive to produce theatre, and government funding is increasingly difficult to access. Theatre critics are often unkind, and, sadly, frequently unin- formed—and there are so few of them. The competition for an audience between the various narrative disciplines is unrelenting. In addition to film and television, gaming technology has gained tremendous popularity.

The mainstream theatres tend to recycle a very few plays that are aimed squarely at their affluent subscription audiences. There are a small

---

\* Matthews, *Papers on Playmaking*, 92.

number of venues that produce works that are truly reflective of the diversity that one sees in the population.

Still the theatre persists. It persists because it is such an alive and elemental form. An argument can be made that it is the most human and humanizing form of literature, in that it is meant for humans to express and consume, and ultimately, when it is fully realized, a live audience will watch other live humans walk, talk, fight, love, get hurt, get healed, and receive comfort within the same room as themselves. If you attend the theatre you must give of your time, your attention, and your imagination. You must sit among other breathing, sweating humans, and you must apply yourself. There is a sense of vitality and energy and authenticity that accompanies this form that cannot be duplicated by any other. It's true that the audience that attends the theatre is tiny, but it's a passionate and outspoken one.

And there is a hunger out there for new voices as there has never been before. If you genuinely have something to say, there is no more active form, no more generous form, no more exciting form than the theatre.

But you can't talk your way there, you can't bluff your way there, and you can't fight your way there. There's only one way to find your way to the audience, and that is to write your way there.

Are you ready? There's work to be done.

# PART TEN
## EPILOGUE

# WRITING ORGANIZATIONS

As you continue writing, you should be aware that there are a number of organizations that exist to provide help, support, and advice for playwrights. Some of these organizations are:

**In Canada**

**Alberta Playwrights' Network**
331 41 Ave. NE
Calgary, Alberta
T2E 2N4
(403) 269-8564 :: trevor@albertaplaywrights.com

**Banff Playwrights Lab**
The Banff Centre
107 Tunnel Mountain Drive
Box 1020, Stn. 43
Banff, Alberta
T1L 1H5
(403) 762-6365 :: performing_arts@banffcentre.ca

**Centre des auteurs dramatiques**
261 Saint-Sacrement Street, Suite 200
Montreal, Quebec
H2Y 3V2
(514) 288-3384 :: cead@cead.qc.ca

## Manitoba Association of Playwrights
503-100 Arthur Street
Winnipeg, Manitoba
R3B 1H3
(204) 942-8941 :: mbplay@mymts.net

## Nightswimming
The Distillery Historic District
15 Case Goods Lane, Studio #310
Toronto, Ontario
M5A 3C4
(416) 504-3898 :: brittany@nightswimmingtheatre.com

## Playwrights Atlantic Resource Centre
PO Box 33038
Quinpool RPO
Halifax, Nova Scotia
B3L 4T6
1-877-845-1341 :: parcoffice@playwrightsatlantic.ca

## Playwrights' Workshop Montréal
7250 Rue Clark, #103
Montreal, Quebec
H2R 2Y3
(514) 843-3685 :: info@playwrights.ca

## Playwrights Theatre Centre
202-739 Gore Avenue
Vancouver, British Columbia
V6A 2Z9
(604) 685-6228 :: plays@playwrightstheatre.com

## Saskatchewan Playwrights Centre
700-601 Spadina Crescent East
Saskatoon, Saskatchewan
S7K 3G8
(306) 665-7707 :: andrew@saskplaywrights.ca

**Playwrights Guild of Canada**
401 Richmond St. West, Suite 350
Toronto, Ontario
M5V 3A8
(416) 703-0201 :: info@playwrightsguild.ca

**In the United States**

**The Dramatists Guild of America, Inc.**
1501 Broadway, Suite 701
New York, New York
10036
(212) 398-9366 :: questions@dramatistsguild.com

**Literary Managers and Dramaturgs of the Americas**
PO Box 586
New York, New York
10108
1-800-680-2148 :: lmdanyc@gmail.com

**In Britain**

**Writers' Guild of Great Britain**
134 Tooley Street
London
SE1 2TU
020-7833-0777 :: admin@writersguild.org.uk

**In Australia**

**Playwriting Australia**
The Arts Exchange
Level 3, 10 Hickson Road
Sydney, New South Wales
2000
(+61) 02 8274 0900 :: info@pwa.org.au

# PLAYS TO READ

Preparing any kind of reading list is dangerous both because of what it may include, as well as what it may ignore. This particular list isn't meant to represent the best of plays everywhere, but only to offer a very arbitrary selection of scripts that may provide a reader with some insights into what playwriting has to offer.

*Accidental Death of an Anarchist* by Dario Fo
*American Buffalo* by David Mamet
*Angels in America* by Tony Kushner
*Antigone* by Sophocles
*Arms and the Man* by George Bernard Shaw
*August: Osage County* by Tracy Letts
*Barungin* by Jack Davis
*A Beautiful Life* by Michael Futcher and Helen Howard
*Betrayal* by Harold Pinter
*The Birds* by Aristophanes
*The Birthday Party* by Harold Pinter
*Blood Relations* by Sharon Pollock
*The Boys* by Gordon Graham
*Brothel #9* by Anusree Roy
*Buried Child* by Sam Shepard
*The Caucasian Chalk Circle* by Bertolt Brecht
*Concord Floral* by Jordan Tannahill
*The Cherry Orchard* by Anton Chekhov

*The Children's Hour* by Lillian Hellman
*Cloud 9* by Caryl Churchill
*The Clouds* by Aristophanes
*The Crucible* by Arthur Miller
*Cyrano de Bergerac* by Edmond Rostand
*Death and the King's Horsemen* by Wole Soyinka
*Death of a Salesman* by Arthur Miller
*Doc* by Sharon Pollock
*A Doll's House* by Henrik Ibsen
*The Drawer Boy* by Michael Healey
*Dry Lips Oughta Move to Kapuskasing* by Tomson Highway
*The Dumb Waiter* by Harold Pinter
*Einstein's Gift* by Vern Thiessen
*Endgame* by Samuel Beckett
*Fences* by August Wilson
*The Frogs* by Aristophanes
*Fool for Love* by Sam Shepard
*for colored girls who have considered suicide / when the rainbow is enuf*
  by Ntozake Shange
*Galileo* by Bertolt Brecht
*The Glass Menagerie* by Tennessee Williams
*Glengarry Glen Ross* by David Mamet
*Half Life* by John Mighton
*Hedda Gabler* by Henrik Ibsen
*Henry V* by William Shakespeare
*Hot L Baltimore* by Lanford Wilson
*The House of Blue Leaves* by John Guare
*How I Learned to Drive* by Paula Vogel
*The Importance of Being Earnest* by Oscar Wilde
*In the Next Room (or The Vibrator Play)* by Sarah Ruhl
*The Island* by Athol Fugard
*Jewel* by Joan MacLeod
*Julius Caesar* by William Shakespeare
*Kim's Convenience* by Ins Choi
*King Lear* by William Shakespeare
*The Laramie Project* by Moisés Kaufman and members of the Tectonic
  Theater Project

*The League of Nathans* by Jason Sherman
*Leaving Home* by David French
*Lion in the Streets* by Judith Thompson
*Macbeth* by William Shakespeare
*"Master Harold" . . . and the Boys* by Athol Fugard
*M. Butterfly* by David Henry Hwang
*Meat Party* by Duong Le Quy
*Medea* by Euripides
*The Miser* by Molière
*Mother Courage* by Bertolt Brecht
*Oedipus Rex* by Sophocles
*Of the Fields, Lately* by David French
*The Persecution and Assassination of Jean-Paul Marat as Performed by the Inmates of the Asylum at Charenton Under the Direction of the Marquis de Sade* by Peter Weiss
*Plenty* by David Hare
*Raisin in the Sun* by Lorraine Hansberry
*The Rez Sisters* by Tomson Highway
*Rhinoceros* by Eugène Ionesco
*Richard III* by William Shakespeare
*Riders to the Sea* by John Millington Synge
*The Rivals* by Richard Sheridan
*Romeo and Juliet* by William Shakespeare
*Rosencrantz and Guildenstern are Dead* by Tom Stoppard
*Ruined* by Lynn Nottage
*Saved* by Edward Bond
*The School for Scandal* by Richard Sheridan
*The Sea* by Edward Bond
*The Seagull* by Anton Chekhov
*Shakespeare's Will* by Vern Thiessen
*The Shape of a Girl* by Joan MacLeod
*Six Degrees of Separation* by John Guare
*Some Assembly Required* by Eugene Stickland
*A Streetcar Named Desire* by Tennessee Williams
*Tartuffe* by Molière
*The Tempest* by William Shakespeare
*Top Girls* by Caryl Churchill

*Toronto, Mississippi* by Joan MacLeod
*Transit of Venus* by Maureen Hunter
*Travesties* by Tom Stoppard
*The Trials of Brother Jero* by Wole Soyinka
*Unity (1918)* by Kevin Kerr
*Waiting for Godot* by Samuel Beckett
*Waiting for the Parade* by John Murrell
*The Weir* by Conor McPherson
*White Biting Dog* by Judith Thompson
*Who's Afraid of Virginia Woolf* by Edward Albee
*Wit* by Margaret Edson
*Zastrozzi* by George F. Walker

As well, there is also a whole body of theatrical works for young people that I would encourage those interested in playwriting to read. The playwrights in this category are so numerous that there is no room to list them all, but there are many plays for young people that are sophisticated, creative, and enchanting.

# GLOSSARY

**Action:** Another term used for the struggle of characters to achieve their desires.

**Actor:** The person who translates the written dialogue and actions of the person imagined by the playwright and physically manifests that character on the stage.

**Antagonist:** The character that most embodies the forces of antagonism within a play. Not necessarily a villain.

**Arc:** The figurative line describing the struggle of the character.

**As the curtain rises:** The beginning of the play. Referencing the moment when the set would be revealed by the opening of the curtain at the beginning of a play. Sometimes shortened to "at rise."

**Backstory:** The historical events that inform a play, but are not necessarily contained, or even mentioned in the play.

**Character:** An individual with a role in a story or a play.

**Climax:** The turning point in the plot of a play where the desire that has driven the play will either be fulfilled or fail. Generally, the moment of greatest tension.

**Complication:** Incidents and obstructions that lead to an intensification of the conflict of the play.

**Conflict:** The struggle between the opposing forces of the play.

**Crisis:** A point of great tension immediately prior to the climax, which is ended once the protagonist chooses to take the action that leads to the climax.

**Critique:** Focused, coherent criticism of a play.

**Designer:** The person who decodes the text and translates it visually for the various design elements of the stage. These elements—costume, lighting, set, and sound—may be assigned to different individuals, or, in certain cases, may fall within the scope of a single designer.

**Development:** The process of "developing" a new play. That process may include written analysis, workshops, staged readings, and even initial, exploratory productions.

**Dialogue:** The conversation between characters in a play.

**Director:** The person who directs the play—who reads the play and discovers a strategy to visually and physically manifest it on stage.

**Distillation:** The process of isolating and selecting certain essential elements of a story that, when employed in a play, will represent the illusion of the entire action.

**Down stage:** In the direction of the front of the stage, toward the audience.

**Dramaturgy:** Analysis and research of a dramatic text. This analysis is sometimes applied to scripts already in production, and sometimes to scripts that are new and in development.

**Exposition:** Information that is necessary to the development of the plot.

**Improvise:** To make up fresh, or generate anew. Any narrative or character elements created without a set script can be said to be improvised.

**Location:** The place or physical environment in which a play or scene of a play is set.

**Monologue:** An extended speech of an individual character.

**Objective:** The acted upon desires and wants of characters.

**Obligatory scene:** The expected and awaited clash between the principal adversaries of a play.

**Parenthetical:** Where there is ambiguity about how a line may be interpreted, a parenthetical instruction may be used to clarify things. Parentheticals are also utilized for line-specific stage directions and these are placed within the dialogue itself, in parenthesis. And thus the name.

**Plot:** A constructed, interconnected series of events based upon principles of cause and effect that guide the characters through the story.

**Protagonist:** The principal character of a script whose acted-upon desire frames and shapes the narrative of the play. Not necessarily heroic.

**Rehearsal:** The process through which actors and a director physically explore the play and define its shape for stage production.

**Resolution:** The portion of the play immediately following the climax that presents the new status quo.

**Reversal:** An action selected by a character that results in the opposite of the intended results, and consequently turns the story in a new direction.

**Rising action:** The defining struggle and conflict of a play in its ascending motion toward greater involvement, greater intimacy, greater candour, and greater stakes.

**Scenario:** A detailed scene-by-scene breakdown of the play, with the description focusing upon the action and struggles of those scenes.

**Scene:** A single unit of action within a play. Sometimes this unit is framed by a change of time or location. Sometimes it is framed by the entrance or exit of a character.

**Setting:** The physical location, or locations, of a play.

**Stage directions:** Specific written instructions provided by the playwright in the body of the script that relate information regarding what the characters are doing, and what is happening on the stage.

**Stage left:** The lateral area of the stage that is on the left-hand side of an actor who is standing on the stage facing the audience.

**Stage right:** The lateral area of the stage that is on the right-hand side of an actor who is standing on the stage facing the audience.

**Status quo:** The world as it is. The present circumstances.

**Story:** A sequence of actions that have a beginning, middle, and end and generally possess a unity of character and theme.

**Subtext:** The unstated, unwritten intentions of your characters that are delivered beneath the obvious and explicit dialogue and actions.

**Through-line:** The major action of a play, distilled.

**Time lock:** A limited time frame that places constraints upon how long characters have to achieve or complete something. If a vampire has to be found before the sun sets, that's a time lock. Placing a time lock on something adds another form of pressure and a level of difficulty to an endeavour.

**Up stage:** In the direction of the rear wall of the stage and away from the audience. Arising out of the days when the stages were raked to improve sightlines, so those who moved toward the rear of the stage were literally "up" stage.

**Workshop:** An activity designed to pay attention to a play, generally to examine some of its more essential elements, the structure, the development of the characters, generally for the purpose of providing the playwright guidance in their rewriting.

# BIBLIOGRAPHY

Beckett, Samuel. *Endgame: A Play in One Act*. New York: Grove Press, 1958.

Cole, Susan Letzler. *Playwrights in Rehearsal: The Seduction of Company*. New York: Routledge, 2001.

Chekhov, Anton. "Anton Chekhov on Writing." Study Lib. https://studylib.net/doc/8482619/anton-chekhov.

---. *Nine Plays of Chekhov*. New York: Grosset & Dunlap, 1947.

Choi, Ins. *Kim's Convenience*. Toronto: Toronto: House of Anansi Press, 2012.

Churchill, Caryl. *Top Girls*. London: Methuen, 1982.

Davis, Jack. *Barungin*. Sydney: Currency Press, 1988.

Durang, Christopher. "Seven Sure-fire Exercises to Lead Your Inner Playwright to Inspiration." *atPlay Newsletter* (Spring/Summer 2005): 11.

Fraser, Brad. *Unidentified Human Remains and the True Nature of Love*. Edmonton: NeWest Press, 1996.

Hemming, Sarah. "Adapting Novels for the Theatre." *Financial Times*, 22 November 2013. https://www.ft.com/content/30392f4c-5130-11e3-b499-00144feabdc0.

Highway, Tomson. *Dry Lips Oughta Move to Kapuskasing*. Saskatoon: Fifth House Publishers, 1989.

Golden, Leon, and O.B. Hardison Jr. *Aristotle's Poetics: A Translation and Commentary for Students of Literature*. New Jersey: Prentice-Hall, 1968.

Johnstone, Keith. *Impro: Improvisation and the Theatre*. London: Methuen, 1983.

Kane, Sarah. *Sarah Kane: Complete Plays*. London: Methuen, 2001.

MacLeod, Joan. *The Shape of a Girl & Jewel*. Vancouver: Talonbooks, 2002.

Martini, Clem. *Illegal Entry*. Toronto: Playwrights Canada Press, 1999.

Matthews, Brander, ed. *Papers on Playmaking*. New York: Hill and Wang, 1957.

McLaughlin, Buzz. *The Playwright's Process: Learning the Craft from Today's Leading Dramatists*. New York: Back Stage Books, 1997.

Pinter, Harold. *The Birthday Party & The Room: 2 Plays by Harold Pinter*. New York: Grove Press Inc., 1961.

---. "Art, Truth and Politics." Nobel Prize, 2005. https://www.nobelprize.org/prizes/literature/2005/pinter/25621-harold-pinter-nobel-lecture-2005/.

Rigg, Diana. *No Turn Unstoned*. London: Arrow Books, 1987.

Roy, Anusree. *Brothel #9*. Toronto: Playwrights Canada Press, 2012.

Sears, Djanet. *The Adventures of a Black Girl in Search of God*. Toronto: Playwrights Canada Press, 2003.

Soyinka, Wole. *Six Plays*. London: Methuen, 1984.

Stickland, Eugene. *Some Assembly Required*. Regina: Coteau Books, 1995.

Stoppard, Tom. "The Bad End Unhappily." American Association of Community Theatre. https://aact.org/bad-end-unhappily-goo.

---. *Travesties*. New York: Grove Press, 1975.

Sullivan, Victoria, and James Hatch, ed. *Plays By and About Women*. New York: Vintage Books, 1973.

Tannahill, Jordan. *Concord Floral*. Toronto: Playwrights Canada Press, 2016.

Thiessen, Vern. *Einstein's Gift*. Toronto: Playwrights Canada Press, 2003.

---. *Of Human Bondage*. Toronto: Playwrights Canada Press, 2016.

Thompson, Judith. *The Crackwalker*. Toronto: Playwrights Canada Press, 1980.

Wilde, Oscar. *The Importance of Being Earnest*. London: Nick Hern Books, 1995.

Williams, Tennessee. *The Glass Menagerie*. New York: Random House, 1949.

# ACKNOWLEDGEMENTS

I would like to acknowledge the assistance of the Killam Foundation for their generous support of this book. I would also like to thank a number of individuals who were helpful in a variety of ways and whose comments and close scrutiny proved invaluable to me: Cheryl Foggo, Chandra and Miranda Martini, Amos Altman, Anne-Marie Bruzga, Ryan Diller, Dr. John Poulsen, Meredith Taylor-Parry, Joan MacLeod, Ken Cameron, Angela Rebeiro, Vern Thiessen, Annie Gibson, Blake Sproule, Alberta Playwrights' Network, and the School of Creative and Performing Arts at the University of Calgary. Many thanks.

The End.

Or the resolution. As you wish.

Clem Martini is an award-winning playwright, novel-
ist, and screenwriter with over thirty plays and twelve
books of fiction and nonfiction to his credit, including
the W.O. Mitchell Book Prize-winning *Bitter Medicine: A
Graphic Memoir of Mental Illness*, the recently launched
*The Unravelling*, and *The Comedian*. His texts on playwriting, *The Blunt Playwright*, *The Greek Playwright*, and
*The Ancient Comedians* are employed widely at universities and colleges across the continent. He currently
teaches in the School of Creative and Performing Arts
at the University of Calgary.

**PLAYWRIGHTS
CANADA PRESS**

202-269 Richmond St. W.
Toronto, ON
M5V 1X1

416.703.0013
info@playwrightscanada.com
www.playwrightscanada.com
@playcanpress